Happy Birthday
M~~ari~~
With ~~much love~~ –
Linda

I pray you continue to grow in the freedom of God's grace & the gospel.

SUPER ^free WOMAN

ENDORSEMENTS

"In a time where self-proclaimed spirituality and theologically erroneous Christian hierarchy run rampant, this work could not have come at a better time. Marci punches holes in our thinking and swiftly pulls the rug out from underneath what we define as "Godly." I have never read a work so inspired, radical, and necessary for this time."
Julianna Zobrist, Christian singer/songwriter and wife of major league baseball player Ben Zobrist.

"As one of Marci's youth pastors, it was both saddening and at the same time incredibly encouraging to read her book. It grieved me deeply to hear how "law/rules/do-this" Christianity had been communicated and what hypocrisy such distortions of Biblical truth created. But to read that through it all, the tenacious pursuing love of Christ was arresting a soul…total delight.

Then I let my wife read it. And she was immediately an enthusiastic endorser! Linda said that Marci has written a "spot-on" work about the unaddressed realities of "do/don't do" expectations imposed upon women seeking to be truly Biblical. She became an instant fan! Marci has obviously identified an "itch" and provided a timely "scratcher"!

May many a "super woman" find new freedom to live the Biblical Christian life by taking time to seriously consider Marci's excellent work!"
Tom Rempel, Senior Pastor of Faith Bible Church, Lincoln, Nebraska

"Revealing, convicting and inspiring. What an incredible message of hope for all women striving to be godly! Marci Preheim provides us with a much needed practical resource for discovering who the truly godly woman is and isn't. Major lies are identified that have held women captive through the years and are replaced with the freedom and truth of God's Word. Here you will find the blending of personal illustrations with biblical insights that reflect her deep commitment to rightly dividing the Word of truth. Marci masterfully reminds women that at the core of godliness, is abiding in Christ, in truth, and in faith. This book will be an immeasurable blessing to every woman who seeks to be godly and to be set free at last from the bondage of conformity to rules and standards set by man, not by God. I highly recommend this book and plan to introduce it to others as I share with women in conferences and retreats across the country."

Marlean Felix, Women's Bible Conference Speaker, Elementary School Teacher, Wife of Seminary Professor Paul Felix, and Mother of Wes and Allyson, Gold Medal Olympian 2012.

SUPER *free* WOMAN

*From Fundamentalist
to Failure to Faith*

MARCI PREHEIM
foreword by Byron Yawn

copyright © 2012 by Marci Preheim.

All rights reserved. No portion of this book may be reproduced, stored in a retrieval system, or transmitted in any form or by any means—electronic, mechanical, photocopy, recording, scanning, or other—except for brief quotations in critical reviews or articles, without the prior written permission of the publisher.

Unless otherwise noted, all scripture verses are from the Holy Bible, New International Version®, NIV®. Copyright © 1973, 1978, 1984 Biblica. Used by permission of Zondervan. All rights reserved worldwide. www.zondervan.com

Scripture quotations marked kjv are from the King James Version.

Back cover author photo by Julie Schepmann

ISBN: 1480210021
ISBN 13: 9781480210028
Library of Congress Control Number: 2012920512
CreateSpace Independent Publishing Platform
North Charleston, South Carolina

Printed in the United States of America

This book is dedicated to my husband Arnie who, second only to Jesus, is the love of my life.

TABLE OF CONTENTS

Forward by Byron Yawn .... *xi*
Introduction: Rules, Rules, Rules .... *xv*

1. Redefining the Godly Woman 1
2. Exposing the Stepford Wives of Evangelicalism 11
3. Will the Real Evil Doer Please Stand Up? 25
4. Sin Management 39
5. A Real Enemy 53
6. Standing Firm 65
7. A Powerfully Mundane Life 77
8. Keeping Your Eyes on Christ in the Storm 89
9. Friendship and the Fear of Man (or Woman) 101
10. The Truth About Women and Men 115
11. Abiding in Humility 129

Acknowledgments *141*

FORWARD BY BYRON YAWN

If the problem with Christian men in the modern evangelical church is a tolerance of their failure to act as men, then the corresponding problem on the other side is the exact opposite – our intolerance of any perceived failure in our Christian women. Our men are in bondage to an extended adolescence that the church has proliferated through low expectations. Our women are in bondage to a form of perfectionism that the church has encouraged through unrealistic expectations. The contrast in what we have come to expect from the genders could not be more stark. The similarity here, however, is also stark: the inability of the church to apply the Gospel as the remedy in both extremes.

The recent call within evangelicalism for men to abandon their negligence has been well and good. There are signs of great progress. The Gospel has begun to take center stage, as well as take root in many hearts. Men have been motivated by the spectacle of grace to *take up* their responsibility and lead. But, where is the corresponding call on our women to *lay down* the burden of performance set on them by the good intentions of the church? Who is calling our women with equal zeal out of their own peculiar bondage to the same grace of Christ? While setting our men free from one prison, have we abandoned our women to languish in another?

If there is one creature in the church of Christ that silently struggles under the weight of performance more than any other, it may well be the wife and mother. The alchemy for hypocrisy found within her Christian duty is greater than most others. Wives and moms can easily keep the true condition of their hearts from view behind unending tasks and domestic responsibilities. The calls to submission and a quiet spirit may well be interpreted by them as prohibitions against any failure or personal weakness. It's suffocating. Women are expected to have it all together. The end result is mechanical, burdensome and joyless womanhood which drones on having forgotten that one thing which rises above all her duties and gives them all meaning – Jesus Christ.

As it is, this burden on Christian women is handed down from generation to generation within the church. This can hardly be denied. Our teaching on womanhood is nearly completely absent of the Gospel of grace. It is nearly exclusively committed to duty. Christian womanhood as propagated by evangelicalism may be reduced down to one extensive and unending "to do list." This type of Christian womanhood barely rises to the level of a sanctimonious home economics course.

Almost all of our biblical teaching boils down to a feminized brand of moralism. Most notable is our use of the Proverbs 31 woman as a template for feminine godliness and self-discipline. Without hesitation we assume the point of the Proverb is to offer a pattern of behavior. To question this interpretation is sacrilege. Think of all the Christian coffee mugs and Kinkade-like prints that bear this emphasis. The assumption is rampant. But is this really the point? In fact, patterning our lives after a fallen human being (even one found in the Bible) is in direct contradiction to the point of the Bible itself – "for all have sinned and fall short of the glory of God." We took what was a poem composed by a doting husband and turned it into a behavioral strategy for godliness.

In this, and many other similar ways, we have robbed women within the church of the sincere joy of Christian womanhood. We have kept them back from grace and true freedom. Godliness comes from a relationship with Christ Jesus and a transformed heart, not a list. To be clear, the aim is not to be liberated from one's responsibilities, to excuse neglect, or deny God's design of male authority. The aim is to be liberated from the tendency to measure self by one's performance in fulfilling the duties one is called to. Our righteousness is outside of us in Christ and not in our relative ability to keep a clean house. It is this latter awareness that liberates one to undertake their duty with complete joy and freedom.

Marci Preheim, believer, wife, mother, servant, friend, congregant and faithful teacher, gets it. By "get it" I mean, gets the Gospel of Christ. Having suffered under the same type of empty moralism herself and having seen its effects in the lives of others, she was finally liberated by the blinding reality of the grace of God in the Cross of Christ. She has in turn made it her mission in life to "free captives" by applying the unending depths of the Gospel to the lives of women. Marci's message has sparked a revolution among the ladies in this congregation I pastor. The result has been a true women's liberation movement. Unlike the ugly outcomes of past movements, the women in this one are not rebelling against the constraints of their God given roles, but embracing them in the freedom which can only come from the personal application of the cross of Christ.

Byron Yawn
Senior Pastor – Community Bible Church
Nashville, TN

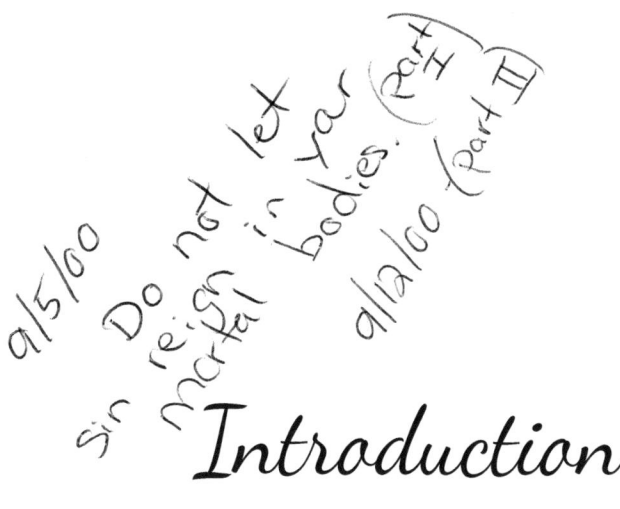

Introduction

RULES, RULES, RULES

Throughout history, the human race has had a propensity to take God's requirements (worship, devotion, and loving obedience from the heart) and reduce them to a list of external rules. From the earliest tribes, even as far back as Adam and Eve's firstborn son, to the present, humanity has always wanted to quantify and qualify our relationship with God—a way to earn His favor, a way to make ourselves godly. We think if we have a set of tangible steps, we will be able to keep them. Success can be charted, rewarded, and checked off the list.

The truth is many have tried to make a workable set of rules for godliness, and the trap that snares so many earnest seekers is the façade of good behavior. I am confident that what originates as an attempt to become godly ends up quenching the power of the true gospel. Women in particular seek this goal. We give each other helpful hints for how to have the perfect quiet time. We share ideas for running our homes efficiently, the best homeschool curriculum and discipline charts for children. In a subtle shift, these good things (and others) over time become human obligations—laws the Lord does not require.

The ancient Israelites tried this, adding many more rules to the ones God had given them in the Law and going through the motions of religion. But God was not pleased. He said they drew near to Him with their lips, but their hearts were far from Him (see Isaiah 29:13). The apostle Paul saw the same thing in his day and predicted it would only become more evident in the last days when people will have a form of godliness but deny its power (see 2 Timothy 3:5).

Modern Christians may look down on the Israelites, but this practice is alive and well in Christian circles today. We have a form of godliness but deny its power most of the time. We have learned to hide our sin rather than repent of it. Nowadays it is commonplace for Christians to form social groups with each other and isolate themselves from the world. I have witnessed Christian women (myself included) neglect God's call to live gospel-centered lives in favor of obedience to Emily Post and to each other. It's almost as if obeying rules of etiquette somehow brings us closer to God.

> "WHEN WE SPEND MORE TIME TRYING TO APPEAR GODLY RATHER THAN ACTUALLY BEING CLOSE TO GOD, THERE CAN BE NO OTHER MOTIVE THAN A DESIRE FOR APPROVAL FROM PEOPLE RATHER THAN FROM GOD HIMSELF."

But the more I learn about abiding in Christ, the less I believe that these activities bring me close to God. In fact, they may actually draw me away from Him.

It is dangerous to overemphasize behavior. Focusing on behavior leads to external works and a neglect of the heart—which is where true godliness is or isn't. Behavior can be manufactured, wisdom cannot. When we spend more time trying to appear godly rather than actually

Rules, Rules, Rules

being close to God, there can be no other motive than a desire for approval from people rather than from God Himself.

I shared my thoughts about this trend with a woman I love and trust. She is suffering with kidney failure and is expecting to see Jesus soon. My dear friend confessed to me that the week prior to my visit she had been too ill to pick up her Bible and have her quiet time. Racked with contrition over this, she cried to the Lord for forgiveness. The heavy hand of man-made law enslaves those who should be enjoying their freedom and close walk with God. Nowhere in the Bible are we given a regiment for daily quiet time as a requirement for keeping God's favor. Later I wept over the needless guilt she suffered and determined in my heart to rip the covers off the shriveled leg of legalism that cripples women's souls.

The book you hold in your hand is the product of that resolve.

Handwritten annotations:

Why is this so wrong to feel guilt over not reading her Bible? Shouldn't we feel something for not reading our Bible?

(Jeremiah feels guilt for not reading)

If we then feel guilty, we didn't do something for the right reasons. We can feel disappointed, but not guilt.

1

REDEFINING THE GODLY WOMAN

What is the definition of a godly woman anyway? Many people esteem the Proverbs 31 woman as the supreme example. I can almost hear a collective sigh as an unattainable list comprised of early mornings and blistered hands comes to mind. This biblically ideal woman's life has been offered as a template, but does merely emulating her behavior make women godly?

If we could interview the Proverbs 31 woman, she would reject all the praise about her and give praise to God instead. She would not point to the things she does, or is able to accomplish in a given day. She would be ashamed of all the fuss we've made over her. She would thank her husband for his encouragement, but admit her inadequacies in her next breath. She would not point to herself or anything she has done. She would point to the grace of God found in the righteous sacrifice of Jesus Christ. She would humbly tell us that in spite of her sin and many failures, God has been gracious to her. When we are not able to keep up with the behavior of the Proverbs 31 woman, we are cordially invited to "approach the throne of grace with confidence, so that we may receive mercy and find grace to help us in our time of need" (Hebrews 4:16).

My whole life I've watched women fall into the same quagmire of conformity. I'm not talking about biblical conformity to the image of Christ, but conformity to an unwritten code of some illusive "godly woman" that doesn't exist. She is subtly different in each church. She dresses a certain way. She has a certain type of personality. She pursues certain hobbies and activities. If her behavior becomes a code to live by in order to be considered godly by the rest of the women in the church, then she is a false gospel. This nonexistent woman robs us of intimacy with each other, condemns us as mothers and wives, and holds us in a prison of law that none of us can live up to. She is a form of godliness that denies the power of the true gospel in women's lives. The godly woman must be redefined in our generation.

Who Invited *Her*?

I grew up in a church where the Bible was taught meticulously. I asked Jesus to come into my heart several times just in case. But a just-in-case prayer is not a prayer of faith. In my elementary years I looked around church and perceived that the more disciplined a woman was, the more godly she was. This perception was solidified in my Sunday school classes, in which we were encouraged to keep daily journals, prayer requests, and memory verses on note cards. Every New Year's resolution incorporated these activities into my daily life. But I was never able to discipline myself for very long. By the middle of January it was proven once again that I was a complete failure.

During my teen years our youth group thrived on lectures about the dangers of rock 'n' roll music and premarital sex. We were given charts instructing us on the progression of fornication. Holding hands was permitted, but kissing was definitely out of the question. We had campfires where we were given the opportunity to burn our sinful music. It always ended with a tearful rendition of "Kumbaya."

As expectations for my behavior grew, my desire to meet them shrunk. Many of my friends in youth group were able to successfully party with the in-crowd at school while maintaining a clean-cut image at church. We had an unspoken code—no one snitches.

Eventually, I lost my desire to keep up with appearances and my parents grew increasingly desperate to control my behavior and hide it from church people. I was grounded every other weekend. My car was taken away. I was forbidden from seeing friends. My mother stood at the door each evening waiting to smell my fingers when I got home to make sure I hadn't been smoking. I learned you don't need fingers to smoke.

My parents tried to preach the Scripture to me but I didn't want to hear it. It all sounded like a bunch of boring rules to me. They told me I was risking their positions of leadership at church and that my behavior was hurting them. I didn't want to hurt my parents but their plea did not motivate me. I thought: *I'm trying to hide it from you so it won't hurt you.*

I believed that Jesus died on the cross for my sins, and since I had prayed several just-in-case prayers when I was young, I was sure I was saved. I didn't need to fake righteousness the way I thought everyone else in youth group was. My parents were the last to know the real depth of my depravity. They were blinded by love for me and a disbelief that their daughter could turn out badly.

At nineteen, I moved to Hollywood. There my lifestyle declined rapidly. There were several situations I put myself into in which God had to supernaturally save my life. However, I did not repent. I pursued my own happiness full time but ironically became increasingly depressed and frustrated. Of course, I believed this was everyone else's fault. I decided to go to church to meet some quality people. There I met a young man who was kind and funny. I pursued him every time I was at church. We became friends.

One Sunday, he grabbed me by the hand and pulled me across the room so we could talk privately. My heart was in my throat. He turned and looked at me and said "Marci, I'm moving to Hawaii for the next two years for college. I want us to write to each other while I'm gone okay?" I agreed and thought: *This is actually perfect. I have two years to clean myself up.* I made a plan to discipline myself to read the Bible, pray, journal, quit smoking, whatever—very soon. However, I did have two years so there was no hurry.

Letters were never exchanged. A few weeks after his departure, news came that he was involved in a diving accident. Then, the great blow—he did not survive. Over the next few months as I grieved alone for my friend, my eyes gradually opened and I began to see my sin. The weight of it was unbearable. There were days I couldn't even get out of bed. I could not figure out why God would take this good man and leave me. I deserved his fate. I had become a hypocrite to impress him. I was the one hiding a mountain of sin—leading a double life.

I cannot nail down an exact date, but during a three-month time frame some dramatic changes took place in my life. I could do little else but read my Bible, weep, and repent. I lost interest in drinking and drugs. I began to listen to sermons on tape to satiate my hunger for the Word. I couldn't believe how I had misunderstood the verses I memorized as a child. I didn't notice how obvious the changes in me were but people at church, and everywhere else, did.

Because of my newfound zeal, I lost all my worldly friends. I even lost most of the friends I had made at church—you know, the kids in the back row. Even with no friends, I wanted to spend all my time at church and with people who would teach me the Word. Through all the years of hearing that I needed to "accept Jesus as my Savior," for the first time I realized I needed to fall flat on my face and beg *Him* to accept *me* even though I didn't deserve it. I still had lingering sin, but as the Lord opened my eyes to it, I did not have to strive to give it up—I hated it. My desires changed daily. I didn't realize it at the time but the false gospel of self-discipline I had grown up believing was now replaced with the true gospel—the gospel of Jesus Christ, who saves sinners.

Those days were lonely but sweet. I felt like it was just me and God and my sermon tapes. I no longer fit in with the world, but didn't quite fit in with church folk either. Regardless, I attended anything and everything offered at church. One weekend I attended a workshop for women. The speaker started talking about what a godly woman does and doesn't do. She said a godly woman doesn't chew gum or skip steps. I looked around to see if anyone was as horrified as I was. Everyone seemed to be eating it up—smiling and scribbling copious notes. She talked about memory verse cards and three-ring binders with prayer requests and how godly it was to rise early in the morning. At intermission I raced to my car, tears burning down my cheeks. That old familiar false gospel of Christian activity was like a crushing weight on my chest. I did not go back to her seminar—I had been saved by the true gospel from my inability to keep all those rules.

Faith or Formula

The lie that presumes etiquette and self-discipline equal godliness has crept into many Biblically solid churches virtually undetected. As I have begun to teach this concept to groups of women, I get the same objection all the time: "But Marci, we have to obey!" It seems to them that I am teaching we don't have to obey God, that we just feel love for Jesus and do whatever we want.

But obedience is not the debate—we all agree that we must obey the Lord. But what exactly are we to obey? This is what has become confusing because over the years, people have added their own rules to what we are to obey—things God does not require.

> "OBEDIENCE IS NOT THE DEBATE—WE ALL AGREE THAT WE MUST OBEY THE LORD. BUT WHAT EXACTLY ARE WE TO OBEY?"

Recently, I read through the entire New Testament and documented every command I could find, beginning in Romans (I left out the narrative passages) and ending with the letters to the churches in Revelation. Skimming through all twenty-five pages of commands, I found that they could all be reduced down to one—abide in Christ. I did not find many activity-based commands that could be written down on a to-do list and crossed off at the end of the day. Maybe you could successfully cross off "do not be drunk with wine" but how would you cross off "but be filled with the Holy Spirit" (see Ephesians 5:18)?

I found commands to "put on the Lord Jesus Christ," to "flee immorality," to "be transformed by the renewing of your mind," and to "watch out for those who cause divisions and put obstacles in your way." These commands reveal God's interest in our hearts and our beliefs—not necessarily our activities. Activities that flow from a heart of faith will vary from person to person. But following rules does not make someone righteous. "If a law had been given that could impart life, then righteousness would certainly have come by the law" (Galatians 3:21).

Genuine obedience to Christ begins with belief. Take, for example, the command to "flee immorality." A woman in the church who everyone perceived as godly was always busy with Christian activity. She homeschooled her children, kept an immaculate house, dressed conservatively, and rarely missed church meetings. Everyone tried to be like her and felt intimidated by her seeming perfection. Her marriage had everyday struggles but was not unusually unhappy. No one would have suspected that this woman was entertaining a flirtation with a man who was not her husband. One day she pulled me aside and confided the allurement to me. The man was exciting, rich, and full of promises. The temptation was great.

She had a choice. She could either believe God or her feelings. Her actions would then follow whatever she chose to believe. God says that immorality is a sin that leads to death and destruction. If she believed Him she would literally flee *from* that illicit relationship. Her feelings made her think the relationship would bring exhilaration, happiness, and an escape from drudgery. If she believed her feelings, she would flee *to* the relationship. Either way, her actions would be a result of what she truly believed. Confessing the temptation to me exposed it and robbed it of power. I listened—sometimes all you need is someone who will listen with compassion and without judgment—and she was able to draw her own conclusions. She saw the trap being laid for her. She repented, *believed* the allurement was a lie, and avoided disaster.

> "THE POWER OF GOD COMES FROM KNOWING AND THEN BELIEVING WHAT IS IN HIS WORD."

Most of us have heard countless sermons on obedience that instructed us to pull ourselves up by our bootstraps (somehow), shape up, and live the Christian life. The power in those sermons is the motivation to outwardly obey out of guilt. The truth is we *can't*!

Without *His* power, no one can behave like a Christian long-term. The power of God comes from knowing and then believing what is in His Word. "Without faith it is impossible to please God" (Hebrews 11:6). We deny God's power when we claim Christianity but only put on an outward appearance of obedience.

As I look back on my childhood with adult (and regenerate) eyes, I see the false gospel that Christian activity preaches. When we start preaching Christian activity more than we preach the gospel, we subtly communicate that God is more pleased with disciplined people—those who are organized, bright, well-behaved, and particularly well put together—and that there isn't much He can do with weak, unorganized, average people. We communicate that God helps those who help themselves. This message causes people to work on the appearance rather than the reality. It causes people to hide who they really are.

I do not blame the church I was raised in that I missed the true gospel for so many years. The Bible states clearly that spiritual things must be spiritually discerned (see 1 Corinthians 2:14). I have no doubt the true gospel was verbally preached hundreds of times during my upbringing—and yet somehow I came away with the idea that Christianity is about lists, rules, and social pressure. Somehow I came away thinking I needed the "Christian seal of approval" from others in the church.

At the heart of the gospel is a recognition of weakness. The Lord saves both the disciplined and the undisciplined alike—the disciplined from trusting in their capabilities and the undisciplined from their sloth. Older Christians somehow forget they didn't cause themselves to mature. Younger Christians feel like they will never attain the level of spirituality they see in others. Everyone wants a formula for godly living, but formula too easily becomes calcified into something that looks like law. To both the disciplined and the undisciplined the Lord says: "Come to me, all you who are weary and burdened, and I will give you rest. . . . My yoke is easy and my burden is light" (Matthew 11:28, 30).

This simple gospel is a gift given to those who *believe* in the finished work of Jesus Christ on the cross and His resurrection—not our own righteousness. Abiding in Christ is not only the secret to being used by God; it is knowing His joy more fully. It sets us free to focus on *one purifying ambition* rather than on a list of rules. That one purifying ambition is to draw near to the Savior by confessing our sins and asking Him to accomplish His work in and through us. It is basking in the freedom of what He has already accomplished for us. Abiding in Christ is the key to our purpose in life, to lasting joy and godly relationships. It's the good news for believers.

[Handwritten note: How exactly do we bask in that freedom? practical steps?]

Making It Stick

- The word *abide* means to stay in a given place, state, relation or expectancy—to continue, dwell, endure, be present, remain, stand, or tarry. The promise to the one who abides in Christ is that Christ will also abide in her (see John 15:4). What do you think Jesus means by this? Is abiding in Christ an inward reality or an outward work? Do any of these potential definitions even remotely resemble a to-do list?

- For further study, read Galatians 3:1–5 to see Paul's response to the Galatians who had fallen into this trap.

Have you found yourself caught up in following rules that have nothing to do with obedience to Christ? Give some thought to when and how you began believing you should follow those rules. Think about what it would be like to be free from social pressure and follow Christ by faith instead.

The "rules" need to get done.
↓
spiritual disciplines

Is the point of this chapter that the spiritual disciplines should be an overflow of our faith rather than a way to achieve God's favor?

If so, how do we make that shift in actions/obedience?

2

EXPOSING THE STEPFORD WIVES OF EVANGELICALISM

The Scriptures call upon older women to teach younger women what is good (Titus 2:3-5). It goes on to give a list of "good" things to teach. In that list of six things, only one is an activity—"to be busy at home." Even that is vague and differs in practicality for each individual. The other five are heart issues: love, self-control, purity, kindness, and submission.

Lots of things can be considered good to busy yourself with at home: homeschooling, crafts, nutrition, home decorating, sewing, housekeeping, couponing, and so on. Are these things what the apostle Paul had in mind when he said "teach what is good"? These things can all be good unless they become the standard for what a godly woman does. We fall short in our calling to teach each other when we only define *good* in domestic

> "IF A WOMAN'S HEART ISN'T AN OVERFLOW OF THE GOSPEL, EVEN HER BEST DOMESTIC EFFORTS CANNOT MAKE HER GODLY."

and external terms. If a woman's heart isn't an overflow of the gospel, even her best domestic efforts cannot make her godly.

In *The Stepford Wives* (first a 1972 novel and later a movie—twice), a society of men find a way to transform their wives into the women they always thought they wanted: beautiful and thin, finely dressed, domestic goddesses, and tigers in the bedroom. These robotic wives have no opinions. They answer "yes dear" to whatever their husbands ask. What the men discover over time, however, is the dissatisfaction of fake relationships based only on externals. In the story, husbands turn their wives into robots. In the church, women do it to each other.

We don't like messy people we can't fix. Our solution is to come up with a code of behavior we can live by and enforce on others. Our motivation for each other is guilt and the fear of man's (or woman's) disapproval. The counsel goes something like this: follow these steps, this is what worked for me; do what I do; what you need is a schedule. The one who will not (or cannot) follow the code is met with a cold shoulder and silent disapproval when her failure is discovered.

> "NO ONE IS MOTIVATED LONG-TERM BY GUILT."

She may be given a charge to "do better" and sent on her way. Worse yet, this unfortunate disciple may pretend to follow the code, hide her failure—and a hypocrite is born. It is in this manner that the church loses her first love. No one is motivated long-term by guilt. Guilt may reach the behavior but it will never reach the heart.

As a new believer, I could not get enough of God's word. I listened to sermons every day on my way to and from work. At home, I plopped down on my roommate's bed and we would talk about all we were learning. His word poured into me and it poured out of me.

Exposing the Stepford Wives of Evangelicalism

A girl from our church asked us to join her on Saturday mornings for a Bible study and we agreed. On the first morning, she gave us our assignments, a schedule of times and with that, a strict order to be on time. She put herself in authority over us and made sure we complied with the rules. She sternly rebuked us when we didn't follow through "excellently." My roommate and I started feeling trapped. The motivation shifted from joyful conversation about the Lord to reports on how well *we* were disciplining ourselves to please her. That study lasted about three weeks.

The Pharisees were guilty of an extreme form of this type of rule making. Their self-righteousness blinded them to their need for a Savior. They added more laws to God's law in order to *appear* more holy. But it got out of hand. They used these laws to impress one another instead of recognizing their inability to obey God from the heart. Jesus said to them, "How can you believe if you accept praise from one another, yet make no effort to obtain the praise that comes from the only God?" (John 5:44). He pleaded with them to recognize Him as their Savior but they refused. Finally Jesus had had enough: "Woe to you, teachers of the law and Pharisees, you hypocrites! You are like whitewashed tombs, which look beautiful on the outside but on the inside are full of dead men's bones and everything unclean. In the same way, on the outside you appear to people as righteous but on the inside you are full of hypocrisy and wickedness" (Matthew 23:27–28). Here we are two thousand years later doing the very same thing.

Depending on Christ's righteousness is the joyful alternative to human achievement. The beauty of the gospel is realized in the humility that admits we have nothing to offer—no righteousness to bring. We know this, but don't live it in front of each other. Instead we try to prove the opposite. Covering our sin and wearing a mask of external righteousness, we fool others into thinking we are godly.

We were not called to be robots. Jesus said in John 13:34–35, "A new command I give you: Love one another. As I have loved you, so you must love one another. By this all men will know that you are my disciples, if you love one another." I cannot truly love someone if I am enslaved to her opinion of me. Learning to love one another as Christ loved is a lifelong endeavor. It requires vulnerability, longsuffering, forgiveness, and a willingness to be misunderstood or hurt so others can see Christ through us. It is genuine when it originates at the cross, overflowing into every relationship and motivating every pursuit. The result is a living illustration of the true gospel. "Having loved his own who were in the world, he now showed them the full extent of his love" (John 13:1).

Abiding in the Vine

Understanding what it means to abide in Christ is so important to the believer that it was the subject of Christ's parting words to His disciples just before His death. He gave them this word-picture so they would remember it through the crisis of His death. He spoke of the dependent relationship of branches to their vine.

> "UNDERSTANDING WHAT IT MEANS TO ABIDE IN CHRIST IS SO IMPORTANT TO THE BELIEVER THAT IT WAS THE SUBJECT OF CHRIST'S PARTING WORDS."

> I am the true vine, and my Father is the gardener. He cuts off every branch in me that bears no fruit, while every branch that does bear fruit he prunes so that it will be even more fruitful. You are already clean because of the word I have spoken to you. Remain in me, and I will remain in you. No branch can bear fruit by itself; it must remain in the vine.

Exposing the Stepford Wives of Evangelicalism

Neither can you bear fruit unless you remain in me. I am the vine; you are the branches. If a man remains in me and I in him, he will bear much fruit; apart from me you can do nothing. (John 15:1–5)

In this analogy there is only one requirement for fruitfulness—to abide (remain) in the vine. As living branches we passively receive everything—salvation, faith, discernment, forgiveness, a righteousness from God (Romans 3:21). "His divine power has given us everything we need for life and godliness through our knowledge of him who called us by his own glory and goodness" (2 Peter 1:3).

The one command to the living branches is to stay connected to the vine. Translation to believers? Continue to believe Christ in faith no matter what happens. "The righteous will live by faith" (Romans 1:17) not by sight. Your faith will be tested to be proven true through various trials (1 Peter 1:6–7). Peter also reminds believers not to be surprised by trials (1 Peter 4:12). Surely Peter never forgot Jesus's words on the night He was arrested: "I am telling you now before it happens, so that when it does happen you will believe that I am He" (John 13:19).

God the Father is the gardener. He is intimately involved not only in the fruit-bearing process but in the relationship of each branch to the vine. He removes the dead branches and He cuts away the worthless parts of the living ones. This pruning process can be painful, yet it is an essential part of God's continual attention and care over our lives. Romans 8:28 teaches us that God works through our circumstances, even the painful (pruning) ones: "And we know that in all things God works for the good of those who love him, who have been called according to his purpose." Therefore even seemingly unhappy things that come our way are good things—even if they *feel* bad. As our circumstances collide with our biblical knowledge, we learn to grab hold of Christ in faith. Through difficult times, our faith will be strengthened as we believe His word and stand firm in Christ's strength.

My Weakness His Strength

About eighteen months after my conversion I met Nora, a chaplain at a women's prison. I was mesmerized by her stories and inquired how I could serve with her in some small way. I just wanted to be with her. She told me that a team from the church visited the prison once a month for a chapel service and I could join them. I signed up the first chance I got.

The team consisted of three people: the teacher, the song leader, and me. I did nothing but observe the first few times. After that I served in small ways. Once I read a scripture. Another time I shared a brief testimony. It was a simple service that included the three of us, Nora, and one hundred prisoners.

One day on the way to or from the prison (I don't remember), the woman who taught the lesson told me she would be stepping away from the ministry. I looked at her with horror. "Who is going to teach the prisoners?" I asked.

"You are," she said.

I didn't know you could say no to stuff like that back then. I was twenty-two years old, and scared to death. I felt the weight of the ministry lift off her shoulders and bear down on mine. I cried to the Lord. I panicked for a whole month. I cried more. I paced. I prayed. I searched my Bible. I scribbled some notes. I cried some more.

I went to the prison. I shared the gospel in all its beautiful simplicity. The response was powerful. That was my first taste of the Lord's power in my weakness. I went back regularly and had the same result each time. Whatever I was learning at the time, I shared with them. Then I met my husband, married and moved to a new city, and left that ministry to another terrified newcomer.

Through that experience the Lord planted a seed of desire in me—a desire to return to that kind of powerful ministry. In my new city, surrounded by all new people, I knew God was calling me to be a Bible teacher but no one else did. As I spent time thinking of the days at the prison, a new seed began to grow in my heart—a seed of pride.

Somehow, I forgot the crying and the praying and the weakness. I began to think it was my giftedness—rather than the power of the gospel—which had brought about that response. Surely if these people had seen me in action at the prison, they would want me to teach here. At the very least they would want my input and wisdom in conducting the various ministries at church. I believed I had the gift of discernment. But what I called the gift of discernment was really a critical spirit, a lack of submission, and pride.

The Lord did not give me a platform for teaching right away. Instead He put me in charge of the nursery and the preschool departments at church. There are some activities we know we need God's help with and others we think we can manage with human wisdom. This was my view of the nursery. How hard could it be? Get volunteers, make a schedule, and call people to remind them—easy. The problem was, no one wanted to volunteer. People didn't show up for their scheduled time. And when I called for reminders, I got excuses for why they needed to be removed from the schedule.

I missed the church service almost every Sunday during those early years and continually fought feelings of bitterness. Not only was I taking care of my own babies every day but I went to church and had to take care of everyone else's too—it wasn't fair. On occasion, I would cry out to God to free me from my bad attitude and my unwillingness to serve. Sometimes, when I felt like I was at the end of my rope, some sweet middle-aged woman would pass by and say: "Go to church, I'll take care of these babies." God bless those women!

One day, I'd had enough. I called everyone I could think of seeking volunteers. Every person said no. I was angry and judgmental. I cried out to the Lord. I said, "What else can I do, Lord? I've tried everything." Here was the lesson I learned at the prison—but didn't think applied to the nursery. God was waiting for me to recognize my weakness before intervening with His strength. In that moment my perspective changed. A burden was lifted. After all, the Lord wasn't asking me to put my head on a chopping block. He was only asking me to serve the children and their parents for a couple of hours a week.

Having found some peace after my little fit at the foot of the cross, I got up and folded laundry. While I was folding laundry I thought about a conversation I'd had earlier with my friend Sarah. *Hey, I haven't called Sarah*, I thought. *I wonder if she would be willing.* I called, and sure enough, she and her husband happily agreed to serve.

My approach changed from that moment on. Rather than calling people to guilt them into service, I began to pray that the Lord would lay the need on people's hearts and bring them to me. If there was a slot I couldn't fill, I knew He was calling me to fill it. He often made me wait until the last minute but my striving ceased. My faith grew. I lived in the book of Isaiah: "In repentance and rest is your salvation, in quietness and trust is your strength. . . . The LORD longs to be gracious to you; he rises to show you compassion. For the LORD is a God of justice. Blessed are all who wait for him!" (Isaiah 30:15, 18).

This story sounds mystical but we can't control people and circumstances. No matter how gifted we are, the Lord wants us to

Exposing the Stepford Wives of Evangelicalism

be mindful of our weakness. We will not be fruitful based on human abilities. The same Lord who fueled my gospel presentation to one hundred prisoners is also the One who lifted my preschool burden and brought Sarah to mind. I learned again to seek Him with all my heart and to be a servant leader. I couldn't take credit for any success—I was dependent on the Lord for everything.

Desperation Versus Discipline

Abiding in Christ comes more naturally to us living branches when we are suffering. Then no one needs to teach us how. Out of sheer necessity, we cling to Him. This is how He teaches us that He can be trusted. This is how our faith is proven. This is where humility is born. If we can learn how to abide in Christ from our times of suffering, then we learn to lean on Him even during times of ease.

My husband has worked in the volatile banking industry for years. He has been laid off several times because of buyouts, reorgs, and downsizing. No matter how many times this has happened, it does not get any easier. We know the refining process that we will face—it is always painful. We envision having to sell our house or move to a new city or drastically change our lifestyle. My husband goes through the fear of being responsible for providing for his family and the what-ifs of an unstable job market. Each time the Lord reveals some unforeseen object that we have put our faith in instead of Him. Each time He reassures us in a deeper way that He can be trusted. We never enjoy the pain from these trials, but we always see the fruit from them.

The entire Trinity is at work in our lives if we are living branches. The Father will prune away all that is worthless and orchestrate our circumstances for spiritual growth. The Son has paid the price for our sins, which allows us to be living branches on His vine. He is now interceding on our behalf at the right hand of the Father. The Holy

Spirit dwells within us, as the nourishing sap, compelling us to draw near to Christ.

Fruitfulness comes from *believing* more, not necessarily *doing* more. As we abide in Christ, fruit is naturally produced. In nature, branches do not strive to produce fruit. The natural product of abiding in the vine is fruit. As long as the branch is attached to the vine, it *will* bear fruit. Remember: "If a man remains in me and I in him, *he will bear much fruit*" (John 15:5, emphasis mine). There are no added conditions.

> "FRUITFULNESS COMES FROM *BELIEVING* MORE, NOT NECESSARILY DOING MORE."

What Should I Do?

Christians are always wondering what to *do*. I get nervous when I hear people talk about methods for spiritual growth, because that is God's work, not ours. People have been trying to *make* themselves righteous for centuries. It doesn't work that way. Yet the human heart craves law. It wants *steps* so righteousness can be measured. It will also try to find every loophole so sin will still fit into the picture. It justifies anger and self-righteousness. But our inability to keep the law is what we were saved from! Paul wrote, "Are you so foolish? After beginning with the Spirit, are you now trying to attain your goal by human effort?" (Galatians 3:3).

If we teach people that it's only acceptable to spend time with the Lord early in the morning—we alienate all the night people who enjoy Him then. Why would we declare every other time of the day ungodly? Rather than spending time with the Lord during her children's naptime, some young mother may give up altogether because she failed to get up early. We've lowered the standard of "pray without ceasing" to "pray at five o'clock in the morning."

Bible reading and prayer are important in the believer's life but what is the motive behind it? Is it discipline for discipline's sake or is it desperation to know Christ? Is it something we should do that we feel guilty about or do we *believe* it is the source of power, encouragement, comfort, and strength that we desperately need? Do we evangelize out of guilt? Why do we journal or memorize scripture or attend Bible studies? Are we pleasing men or God? The means so easily become the end.

It is by God's grace that any of us hunger and thirst for His righteousness. Desperation draws us to desire Him. If we have to discipline ourselves against our will to draw near to the Lord, then there is a bigger problem than lack of discipline. There's a crisis of faith. There's an arrogance that *believes* there's no urgent need for His power. *Thanks for saving me, I've got it from here, Lord.*

As we draw near to Christ *He* bears the fruit through us. We can dream big as we think about how we would like to participate in the kingdom of God, but we have to let the Lord put us there. We too often go to one extreme or another. Either we think we can't do anything for God (let alone "great things") because we evaluate our limitations, or we think too highly of ourselves and try to serve God in great ways but do so in our flesh. Neither brings about the supernatural fruitfulness that only comes from God's power.

A Body, Not a Business

The body of Christ is not a corporation. We don't all follow the same path, beginning in the mailroom, and retiring fifty years later as honored leaders. Each of us are uniquely gifted at the moment of conversion. Every believer follows an individual path that has been laid out in advance for a specific purpose—to glorify God (Ephesians 2:10).

There is no place for selfish ambition in the church. We don't decide what we will do for God or what our gifts will be. Hard work does not guarantee a position in leadership nor does a life characterized by strict discipline always equate to greater usefulness. Knowledge does not qualify people for leadership—love does. In general, ministries that are run by human wisdom reap only human results—no matter how gifted the leader. Obedience that comes from anything other than faith is legalism. It will not produce "fruit that will last" (John 15:16). It will not persevere. It will not save. "Everything that does not come from faith is sin" (Romans 14:23). When the gospel ceases to be pure and central, the church loses her first love and her power.

> "THERE IS NO PLACE FOR SELFISH AMBITION IN THE CHURCH."

The apostle Paul spent his life planting churches and revisiting them, reminding them to get the gospel right. We so easily get carried away by new trends and marketing schemes in the church. But our first priority is to teach God's Word—pure, undiluted—lest the false teaching of human achievement creeps in. People have died for the purity of the gospel. It is the only battle worth dying for.

I put my testimony in this book for one reason: to reveal the power of the gospel as it is administered through human weakness—both to save and to sanctify. I have the same story as innumerable others who supposedly came to Christ as children (with just-in-case prayers), walked away as teens, and finally in adulthood came to believe in the true gospel of grace alone, through faith alone, in Christ alone.

Throughout your Christian life God shows you how much you need Him. As you learn to depend upon Him, He gives you responsibility, which causes you to depend even more on Him. "Whoever can be trusted with very little can also be trusted with much, and whoever is dishonest with very little will also be dishonest with much" (Luke 16:10). Whatever you are called to do in the body of Christ will become clear as you draw near to Him. You will only be able to persevere if you do it by faith. It is noble to aspire to be an overseer (1 Timothy 3:1), but God has to put you there. We don't make ourselves godly by doing lots of stuff.

God said to Paul, "My grace is sufficient for you, for my power is made perfect in weakness." Paul understood: "Therefore I will boast all the more gladly about my weaknesses, so that Christ's power may rest on me. That is why, for Christ's sake, I delight in weaknesses, in insults, in hardships, in persecutions, in difficulties. For when I am weak, then I am strong" (2 Corinthians 12:9–10). These words are just as true today.

Making it Stick

- "It was a blessing in disguise." How often have you said these words, or had them said to you? Learning to welcome adversity seems counterintuitive. Yet the power in suffering lies in the *belief* that God is doing something good even if it doesn't *feel* good. What good things have come from adversity in your life? What do Romans 5:1–5 and 8:18–25 reveal about our hope through suffering?

- Do you evaluate your limitations and feel disqualified for service or do you feel like you have to be in control because no one will be able to meet your standards? Think about which extreme most describes you. Most of us have struggled at one time or another with both.

- It's important for women to have friendships across many generations; each has something to offer the other, as Paul noted in his letter to Titus. If you are an older woman, is there a younger woman within your purview to whom you might open your heart? Try to let your relationships unfold naturally. Remember, there are no rules!

3

WILL THE REAL EVILDOER PLEASE STAND UP?

One of the most frightening passages in the Bible is Matthew 7:21–23: "Not everyone who says to me, 'Lord, Lord,' will enter the kingdom of heaven, but only he who does the will of my Father who is in heaven. Many will say to me on that day, 'Lord, Lord, did we not prophesy in your name, and in your name drive out demons and perform many miracles?' Then I will tell them plainly, 'I never knew you. Away from me, you evildoers!'"

The evildoers in these verses are religious people. They are people who put their faith in Christian activity (even done in Jesus's name) but missed the Christian faith altogether. The scariest thing about this passage is that it reveals the prevalence of self-deception: "*Many* will say to me on that day . . ."

> "CAN YOU IMAGINE A MORE HORRIFYING DISCOVERY THAN TO STAND BEFORE THE GATES OF HEAVEN FULLY EXPECTING TO GO IN, BUT INSTEAD BEING TURNED AWAY FOR ETERNITY?"

25

It is possible to believe you are a Christian because of your Christian activity and to *not be a Christian*! Can you imagine a more horrifying discovery than to stand before the gates of heaven fully expecting to go in, but instead being turned away for eternity?

The most dangerous aspect of self-deception is that no one believes herself capable of it. And so the deception continues. If questions arise in her heart, she deceives herself into thinking no investigation is necessary (see 2 Corinthians 13:5). In addition to believing the lie that Christian activity validates faith, people also mistakenly equate Biblical knowledge with godliness. God is not pleased with knowledge or activity if they are coupled with spiritual pride. He gives His grace to the humble (James 4:6, 1 Peter 5:5). *This is exactly what I do! I measure Mike's human efforts.*

It is foolish to seek assurance of salvation by human measures or from other people rather than from God's Word. Because we are so easily deceived, James exhorts us to look "intently into the perfect law that gives freedom, and [continue] to do this, not forgetting what [we have] heard" (James 1:25).

Angry and Righteous?

When did it become okay for Christians to be angry people? The anger of religious people seems to grow with the decline in our culture. Sin is discussed more openly these days. It's in our faces day after day. It's all over the news. Even against our will, we have to address it. Every night while I'm cooking dinner, I see commercials on television about erectile dysfunction. My kids ask me what that means! How dare the world be so . . . worldly! We try hard to get people to conform to our Christian standards but they won't cooperate! It makes us so angry that those sinners are ruining our perfect Christian utopia.

My mom visited a few years back when I started doing a little more public speaking. We talked about my tumultuous teenage years and all that she and my dad went through during that time. She knew I had been sharing my testimony with many people and felt like, of all people, she should know my story. I told her I didn't think she would be able to handle it. I understand that protective "mom" thing, since I'm a mom too. But she insisted, so I shared a few stories. Sure enough, she got mad at me as if I had done those things the day before: "Marci, how could you? I never did any of those things when I was your age. In my day those things weren't even socially acceptable."

I understand my mom's fear, her worry about what could've happened—and that her love for me fuels those strong protective feelings. I did do a lot of stupid things. But maybe it was because of social pressure in the '50s that my mom never committed any of those heinous sins. She didn't know the Lord in her teens. She was motivated by social standards. She doesn't understand why I couldn't just behave like she did. I challenged her by asking: do we preach a gospel of social pressure that forces certain behavior, or do we preach the good news about a Savior—Jesus Christ—who died and rose again to reconcile sinful people to God? After a thousand conversations, my mom is getting to the place where she understands that I *had* to fall that far in order to look up and see the gospel that saves *sinners*—not people who think they are good enough.

The first self-righteous angry person shows up in the Bible as early as Genesis chapter 4. Cain was religious. He was angry when God accepted Abel's sacrifice but not his. He wanted to bring the fruit of *his* labor for God's approval rather than bring what God required. Likewise, the prodigal son's older brother was angry when their father welcomed back his sinful brother. He did not realize he too was a prodigal in his heart. When Jesus walked the earth He encountered many angry self-righteous people. In fact, they are the ones who killed him. They wanted credit for their good behavior. These religious people turned their noses up at sinners and condemned Jesus for hanging out with them.

I recall being a new convert and meeting another repentant sinner at Bible study. He and I stood out in that clean-cut group of people—each of us having traces of our past still showing up in our appearance. Jerry had been involved in a homosexual lifestyle. He'd contracted AIDS, which, back then, meant he wasn't going to live very long. Being faced with the reality that he would stand before Jesus soon brought him to repentance and therefore to Bible study. He wanted to grow close to God with the time he had left. After a while, though, Jerry stopped attending Bible study and eventually left our church altogether. I never got to know Jerry very well because of my own baggage, but I heard from someone else that as he neared death he turned to the homosexual community for compassion, having found none at church.

I don't know how true those accusations are but I do know the tendency of the human heart: we compare ourselves to others. It is easy to look at someone else and think he is getting what he deserves—while we ignore the reality of what we deserve. We become accustomed to God's grace so much that we begin to feel entitled to it. We fall into the mentality that we have earned it by our "good behavior" and others must earn our compassion by their good behavior.

> "WE BECOME ACCUSTOMED TO GOD'S GRACE SO MUCH THAT WE BEGIN TO FEEL ENTITLED TO IT."

To some who were confident of their own righteousness and looked down on everybody else, Jesus told this parable: "Two men went up to the temple to pray, one a Pharisee and the other a tax collector. The Pharisee stood up and prayed about himself: 'God, I thank you that I am not like other men—robbers, evildoers, adulterers—or even like this tax collector. I fast twice a week and give a tenth of all I get.' But the tax collector stood at a distance. He would not even look up to heaven, but beat his breast and said, 'God have mercy on me, a sinner.' I tell you that this man, rather than the other, went home justified before God. For everyone who exalts himself will be humbled, and he who humbles himself will be exalted." (Luke 18:9–14)

This tax collector understood something the Pharisee did not. He understood the magnitude of his sin and therefore his need for a savior. Self-righteousness blinds us to our need for the gospel. It blinded this Pharisee to the fact that, like the tax collector, he also had a mountain of sin. Just because social pressure had kept him from acting upon what was in his heart didn't mean he was innocent. If he had understood that sin goes deeper than activity, he would have huddled in the corner and begged for forgiveness too.

Growing up I encountered many angry people who admonished me to stop my bad behavior. But I don't recall anyone ever telling me I couldn't. Some Christians wore their anger as a badge, smiling smugly after they had bulldozed someone into proper behavior. I have been yelled at by teachers and pastors and "godly women." I think rebellious kids see the worst side of "mature" Christians—a side these grownups would never let other people in the church see. (There was one youth pastor who tried to reach me with love. He came to

Super(free)Woman

our church in my junior year of high school. Even though I wasn't willing to give up my sin at the time, I felt safe admitting it to him and listening to his counsel. He didn't try to control me with anger—he just put the gospel in front of me and invited me to lay hold of it.)

Maybe we have forgotten that in Paul's description of love in 1 Corinthians 13:4-5, he only uses two words to define what it is: Love is *patient*. Love is *kind*. His description of what love *isn't* is even more incriminating: "It does not boast, it is not proud. It is not rude, it is not self-seeking, it is not easily angered, it keeps no record of wrongs." Controlling someone with anger may successfully change her behavior for a while. But it will never reach her heart. Likewise, parents who dominate their children into certain behavior may succeed in getting them to comply, but over time their hearts will become embittered. They will only comply until they find a way to escape.

Let's Force Them Into Faith

I think sometimes we view evangelism in a similarly wrong way. Somewhere along the way we have adopted the idea that if Christians can talk louder and be more obnoxious than the culture, people will start listening to us and repent. Maybe we can force them to see things our way. Until a few years ago my definition of a good evangelist was someone who was brave enough to corner some unsuspecting non-Christian and trap her until she mumbled something resembling a sinner's prayer. I remember watching this take place as a kid and hearing people comment to each other how bold so-and-so was with the gospel. I was wrong. Evangelism must begin with love—or it is worthless (1 Corinthians 13:1-3).

When I was pregnant with my first child I went to what's called a birthing class. The best thing to come out of that class was a lifelong friend. Elizabeth and I did not become close until a couple of months after our children were born and our class was long over. I ran into her at Walmart. We *oooh*ed and *ahhhh*ed over each other's infants for a while and then Elizabeth looked at me and blurted out: "I need a friend. Here's my number—can we get together?" Her eyes filled up with tears as she told me that her husband traveled most of the time for his work and she was lonely as she didn't have any family nearby.

I immediately took this as a sign from God that I was to evangelize her. She moved to the top of my prayer list and became "my project." Elizabeth and I did a lot together. She called me to go out to breakfast, to go shopping—she even called when she was on her way to the grocery store just to see if I wanted to tag along. Every time we got together I determined to turn the conversation to the gospel.

The thing about Elizabeth is, she's a master of subject changing. We would get to it every now and then but we would never park there for very long. One day, I decided I was just going to *make* it happen. I didn't care what direction the conversation went, I was going to get back to the gospel. We ordered some cheap Chinese food at the mall and sat at a small table in the food court. Breaking open my egg roll, I started in on my rehearsed speech: "Elizabeth, if you were to die tonight . . ." Just then, a woman passed by us with a tray full of Chinese food and tripped right by our table. Food went flying everywhere and the woman seemed hurt. I was annoyed. I just knew Satan was nearby sticking his foot out to distract the gospel. I had Elizabeth's full attention but my five-step gospel presentation was thwarted . . . again.

Elizabeth jumped from her chair. "Oh you poor thing! Are you okay?" she said, running to the lady's side. Only then did I think maybe I should help too. To my shame, I don't even remember what happened to the woman who fell. I only remember my frustration at not being able to share the gospel with Elizabeth.

Super(free)Woman

As time went on, I grew to love Elizabeth as a dear friend. She came to church with me often. I gave up on giving her the canned presentation I had planned that day, but continued to pray for her and looked for opportunities to talk to her about the Lord. Mostly those opportunities came as I just shared my life with her.

In all of my adult days on this earth, there is one that stands out as . . . sacred. I will never forget it. It all began when Elizabeth found out that her husband had become involved with another woman on a business trip. This woman was shameless. She began stalking Elizabeth and harassing her. If that's not bad enough, she confronted Elizabeth in random public places, causing her to fear going out. Finally, the courts had to get involved. When it was all said and done, Elizabeth and her husband had to pay a humongous sum of money (money they didn't have) to make this woman go away.

I spent more time with Elizabeth than ever before. She wanted me to read scripture to her just so she could get her mind off her fear and her rage. I bumbled around reading a Psalm here and a Proverb there. For the first time in my life, I was at a loss for words. She always said she would leave her husband if she ever caught him cheating. She was so hurt and so angry, I could not imagine this marriage ending any other way. After some counseling with an older couple in our church, however, Elizabeth decided to forgive her husband. To say you forgive someone is one thing—to be able to do it is another.

> "TO SAY YOU FORGIVE SOMEONE IS ONE THING— TO BE ABLE TO DO IT IS ANOTHER."

On this particular day, Elizabeth's husband called and asked me to come over. Elizabeth was screaming and throwing things, and he was concerned about the expletives the children were hearing coming out of their mommy's mouth. Truthfully, I didn't want to go. What could I say? How do I know I wouldn't be that angry? What more scripture could I read to her? But I went. By the time I got there she was hiding under her covers in the back bedroom. I felt so weak and helpless, but I went back there and got in on the other side of the bed. We just laid there—she sobbed silently.

Finally, after what seemed like an eternity, I laid my hand on her arm and started praying. I don't even know what I prayed but when I was done I turned to her and said, "I think you should pray." I had never heard Elizabeth pray but surprisingly, she started eking out some semblance of a prayer. What came next was nothing less than supernatural. I can't even describe it well enough to do it justice. There in the dark, Elizabeth, who I had been praying for forever, began repenting of her *own* sin. Her husband's sin had brought her unconscionable pain but she didn't even bring that up. The Holy Spirit's presence in that room made me tremble so violently I hoped she wasn't distracted by it. I have never witnessed anything so powerful before or since. It was almost as if the curtain was pulled back a little so I could see the bloodied battlefield of good and evil fighting for my friend's soul.

She was changed after that night and so was I. All of my striving and scheming to manipulate my friend into saying some contrived prayer seemed so foolish to me now. What I thought was Satan hindering my gospel presentation I now know was God—holding my tongue until He had prepared the soil of her heart to receive the seed of the gospel. The difference in this form of evangelism from all the "programs" I have learned about is *love*. I had earned the right to share the gospel with Elizabeth in her darkest hour because *she knew I loved her* and even though I did so very poorly—it was the Lord who revealed it to her.

If we focused on abiding in Christ, He would give us His love for others. We wouldn't waste our time trying to come up with clever speeches and manipulative methods. Our mode of evangelism would change. Our idea of who is and who isn't a good evangelist would change and every believer would be empowered with what *should* fuel the gospel—love.

Gospel-Centered Programs or Program-Centered Gospel?

We Christians so easily lose sight of our first love and become preoccupied with programs. When this happens the gospel can die off in one generation. The people in the Ephesian church had been radically saved out of witchcraft and goddess worship. Ancient Ephesus was a hub of temple prostitution. The temple to Diana (also known as Artemis) was one of the Seven Wonders of the World. She was a goddess of fertility and the worship of her centered around the debauchery of sexual extremes and drunken revelry.

The first Christians in Ephesus were so zealous for the gospel that they burned their sorcery books in the public square. This act was not only a bold proclamation of their faith but a serious financial sacrifice. Those books were worth a fortune. They didn't care. They had been set free from the bondage of their sin. Their love for Christ burned brightly—literally. They knew the depth of their depravity and therefore understood the depth of forgiveness and grace they had received.

Over time, they became the most well-taught church in the entire region. The apostle Paul himself spent over two years there. They also had Apollos, Timothy, Aquilla and Priscilla, Tychicus, and most theologians believe the apostle John lived there before he was exiled to the island of Patmos.

How ironic it is, then, that only a couple of decades after the famous book burning, they got a letter from Jesus Himself saying,

Hey, I appreciate all your hard work but you have lost your first love (see Revelation 2:1–7). They had busied themselves so much with Christian activity, no one seemed to notice the power of the Holy Spirit slip out the back door.

Our church partners with a church in the Siberian territory of Russia, and several of our pastors and elders have visited that church to teach and encourage the believers there. That place is a wasteland of freezing temperatures and hopeless alcoholic people. Right in the middle of all that is a little band of Christian warriors. It seems like everyone who comes back from there has a renewed sense of passion for the Lord and His people and a realigned perspective on what's truly important. Many of us want to visit just to catch a bit of their passion. I asked one of the pastors who went what it is about that place that has such an impact on everyone who visits. He said, "All they have is each other and their Bibles." And it's enough! They don't have the luxury of awesome teaching, Bible conferences, many people to choose friendships from, buildings, programs, children's ministry, or marriage counseling . . . but they are *rich*. They have a single-minded focus on Christ, and they truly love each other.

When we lose our first love—which is Christ—our first love becomes *ourselves*. And when we lose our first love, then we definitely lose our second—His people. Christians easily forget that they're on the same team. The people in the Ephesian church had lost sight of what they had been saved from. They thought they were raising their children to be moral people, Christians who

> "WHEN WE LOSE OUR FIRST LOVE—WHICH IS CHRIST—OUR FIRST LOVE BECOMES *OURSELVES*. AND WHEN WE LOSE OUR FIRST LOVE, THEN WE DEFINITELY LOSE OUR SECOND—HIS PEOPLE."

would continue the church, but the gospel so easily gets lost when the focus becomes making people behave. Parents assume their children understand the gospel if they put up a good moral front. But raising children with the idea that they can make themselves righteous with rules for behavior kills the gospel that clearly proclaims the opposite. It is a subtle shift with deadly consequences. We are called in Scripture to discipline our children into proper behavior but the purpose of the law is not to make us righteous but to reveal our sin and to lead us to Christ (see Romans 7:7–8, Galatians 3:19–24).

Returning to Your First Love

There were three instructions the Lord gave this congregation who had lost their first love: remember, repent, and return. The first instruction was to "remember the height from which you have fallen" (Revelation 2:5). The Ephesian church originated with folks who knew their capacity for sin. As their behavior changed, so did their memory of their depravity. We are all depraved. The Bible says: "There is no one righteous, not even one" (Romans 3:10).

One evening in a Bible study I taught on this very subject. A young woman came up to me and said something like: "I have never really done anything that bad. It's hard for me to understand that I'm just as bad a sinner as anyone else." I gave her a very grave challenge. I told her to ask God to reveal to her what she had been saved from. I know from experience that God answers that prayer, and it is never pretty. It is through His mercy, that He reveals our sin to us so that we can repent of it and be healed. The psalmist says, "Search me, O God, and know my heart; test me and know my anxious thoughts. See if there is any offensive way in me, and lead me in the way everlasting" (Psalm 139:22–24). The Lord did reveal this woman's sin—and not just to her. Nothing blinds us like our own pride.

The second command was to repent. Repentance is the cure for pride, which is at the root of all other sin. Our society (and even our churches) trains us to cope rather than repent. Rather than repenting of anger, we justify it, entertain it, blame it on others, and end up passing it on to our kids. We distract ourselves with diversions and coping mechanisms. I used to vacuum when I was struggling with anger. Vacuuming my house made me feel like I was accomplishing something, putting something in order—even if every other area of my life was in disarray. But we are not in control—especially over other people. The angst we feel is our unwillingness to surrender our situation to God and humble ourselves before Him. We want to figure out a solution rather than wait upon Him. I have learned when I am struggling with these feelings to leave my vacuum in the closet and repent of my sin so the Lord can take it away. I may "cast all [my] anxiety upon him because he cares for [me]" (1 Peter 5:7). If I am not abiding in Christ, I am trying to control.

> "REPENTANCE IS THE CURE FOR PRIDE, WHICH IS AT THE ROOT OF ALL OTHER SIN."

The final command was return. The concept of *return* is implied in the words *do the things you did at first*. The interesting thing about this command is that these Ephesian believers were "doing" all sorts of things. What had changed was their motivation. This happens so easily in the church. We stop being motivated by love for Christ and become motivated by guilt from others. Fear of man eventually leads to resentment and disillusionment. Living for human approval is unsatisfying because you can never attain it. Christ called the Ephesians to humble themselves and return to love so radical it was willing to burn its sin in the public square.

Making it Stick

- What makes you angry? What does anger *not* bring about, according to James 1:19–21? Are you tempted to control other people with anger? What is the result? How do you react to people who try to control you with anger? If your reaction is compliance on the outside, what is your internal reaction?

- What is your method of evangelism? Do you feel guilt for not sharing the gospel as often as you should? Do you think guilt is a good motivation for evangelism? How do you think drawing near to the Savior could motivate you to be a better evangelist while at the same time setting you free from scheming and striving to make sure God saves your loved ones?

4

SIN MANAGEMENT

One Sunday morning at church I was working in the nursery. We had one of those nurseries with the half-door that allowed me to see into the sanctuary while at the same time keeping the little ones in. In between welcoming newcomers and signing children in, I took a moment to scan the sanctuary. My eyes rested on a very familiar face. It took a minute for me to realize that I hadn't seen that familiar face in many years. From my post, I called out to her joyfully, "*Leslie!*" I riffled through my memories to recall the last time I'd seen her. Leslie and I grew up together in the same church. We spent a lot of time together, especially in our teenage years. We rebelled together and then lost touch when I moved to California. I was as shocked to see her in church as she was about to be when she saw me.

She hadn't noticed me yet. I started biting on my cuticles (a nervous habit of mine since my youth), realizing what her presence in my church could mean. <u>You can hide a lot of sin by moving away and starting over somewhere new.</u> I had shared my testimony with many people at church but here was a witness. She could tell stories. Details of my sinful past were at her disposal. When I finally got her attention, we shared a surprised and then hesitant smile—both of our minds filing through memories we might rather forget. I could tell she had the same thoughts I had. She was happy to see me, curious how I made it back to church, and hopeful I wouldn't tell people what I knew about her.

When you do not have the power of the Holy Spirit working within you, sin management is all you have. Sin management is putting up a good moral front and managing your sin by hiding it from people rather than confessing it to the Lord. Growing up, Leslie and I (and many others in our youth group) loved our sin. We didn't want to give it up. We learned to manage it with external goodness and keep it from those who demanded good behavior. Sin management only works as long as you can keep it hidden. Neither Leslie nor I were ever very good at hiding our sin. I thank God for that. If I was able to hide my sin, I might still be enslaved to it, just as the Bible tells us.

> This is the verdict: Light has come into the world, but men loved darkness instead of light because their deeds were evil. Everyone who does evil hates the light, and will not come into the light for fear that his deeds will be exposed. But whoever lives by the truth comes into the light, so that it may be seen plainly that what he has done has been done through God. (John 3:19–21)

Since that first meeting at church, Leslie and I have had many lunches, comparing stories over the years we were apart and how the Lord brought us each to repentance. She and I still sit for hours and sort through the false gospel we both believed growing up. We marvel at God's graciousness to draw both of us separately and then bring us back together. We wonder about our peers who did some of the same

Sin Management

stuff we did but were able to hide what we could not. Did they ever come to understand the true gospel, or are they still striving under the bondage of sin management?

Both Leslie and I default to a "striving" mode when we are not consciously believing the true gospel. It's in our DNA to feel like we are not praying hard enough, reading enough scripture, or doing enough godly things to evoke God's favor. We fall into the mentality that somehow with Christian activity we can draw down God's favor upon us. Believing we have His favor whether we perform well in a given day or not is the hardest thing for us to do.

Devotion, Desire, and Dependence

It's dangerous to discuss the "how-to" of abiding in Christ because we may be tempted to get our pens and paper and make a list of activities *we think* will make us godly. When tempted, we need to remind ourselves that abiding is a heart issue, not an activity. Don't get me wrong. True faith does result in acts of righteousness. But righteous works apart from faith are worthless before God. No one seeks God naturally (see Romans 3:11). The desire (the want to) and the ability (the way) to abide comes from Him: "For it is God who works in you *to will and to act* according to his good purpose" (Philippians 2:13, emphasis mine).

> "WE NEED TO REMIND OURSELVES THAT ABIDING IS A HEART ISSUE."

The prophet Ezekiel gives the best description of what God does when He takes over a person's life. This is exactly what happened to me years ago when I finally saw my sin and repented of it. I was not able to change myself. "I will sprinkle clean water on you, and you will be clean; I will cleanse you from all your impurities and from all

41

your idols. I will give you a new heart and put a new spirit in you; I will remove from you your heart of stone and give you a heart of flesh. And I will put my Spirit in you and *move you* to follow my decrees and be careful to keep my laws" (Ezekiel 36:25–27, emphasis mine).

Faith is invisible. Jesus compares it to the wind (see John 3:8). Only the effects of faith can be seen by others. However, since these effects can be fabricated to impress others, I must evaluate myself on the genuineness of it. Here are some illustrations that help me determine if I am abiding in Christ or deceiving myself with Christian activity. Maybe these three descriptions will be helpful to you. They are devotion, desire, and dependence.

Devotion

True devotion is best described to women in the form of romance. In the first few months of young love, it is not difficult to be devoted to that special person. Acts of affection come easily from a heart that is consumed with adoration. That person is the subject of our thoughts 24/7 and we dream of ways to show it outwardly.

I find another simple illustration of devotion when I look at my dog. She is so devoted to me that when she is locked out of the room, she will cry at the door until I let her in. The first thing she does in the morning is come over to my side of the bed and jump up so she can catch a glimpse of me and perhaps even lick my feet if she can get to them. Whether I have been gone five minutes or five hours, I get the same enthusiastic welcome from her when I walk in the door. She did not require lessons in devotion. No one taught her how or when to do it.

Most of us know what devotion is. Why, then, when we talk about "doing our devotions," do images of dry reading and empty prayers come to mind? The Lord wants us to be devoted to Him from the heart.

True acts of devotion originate there. Matthew 6:33 (KJV) says: "Seek ye first the kingdom of God, and his righteousness; and all these things shall be added unto you."

God calls us to seek Him first. We have all heard sermons on rising early to have our "quiet time" to start our day off right. Though that is not a bad idea, it is not required. What He is telling us here has nothing to do with chronological time. He wants us to seek Him *first* as a *priority*. Each of us makes time for what is really important to us. Jeremiah 29:13 says, "You will seek me and find me when you seek me with all your heart."

Devotion is not something we can muster up. When we don't feel devoted, we can confess that and ask the Lord to give us a more devoted heart. And He will. I remind myself that the Bible calls us wandering sheep for a reason. Even when we have enjoyed blessing after blessing because of close fellowship with the Lord, we tend to forget and wander back to our own selfish goals. What we are devoted to is what gets our time and energy. Examining those two things is a good place to begin a personal appraisal of faith.

> "WHAT WE ARE DEVOTED TO IS WHAT GETS OUR TIME AND ENERGY."

Desire

If it sounds like I have mastered the devotion part of abiding in Christ, I need to confess something. There are times I find myself not caring about being fruitful. I lose my desire to stay close to Christ; I selfishly want to pursue my own agenda and fleshly desires. I may even go through the motions of prayer or Bible study with the idea of crossing it off my list for the day so I can get back to doing my own thing. As a result of this phony devotion, as time goes on, my heart begins to harden to the things of God, and I start to act out what has collected in my heart instead—whether that's irritability, ungratefulness, selfishness, or something else.

My kids are usually the first to notice that I am not abiding because I become irritated and impatient with them. Nowadays, they point it out: "Mom, maybe you should go spend some time with Jesus!" What a clue that my heart has wandered away! The longer I let my anger go unchecked, the more damage I do to the ones I love. Once I recognize what I'm doing I have learned to run, not walk, to my Lord's presence and ask Him to cleanse me, to forgive me, and to mold me into His image. I also ask Him to protect my family from the damage my sin causes.

When a desire for Christ wanes, the evidence reveals itself in our behavior and ultimately in bondage to those behaviors. Some people, like me, give in to selfish anger. For some it shows up as paralyzing fear; some grow increasingly depressed and lazy, living in denial of their sin. Drunkenness or other escape methods may follow. These are the manifestations of heart issues that we have become very good at hiding from others. Psalm 37:4 says "Delight yourself in the LORD and he will give you the desires of your heart." This verse does not imply that God will fulfill our selfish desires and instantly give us a new Corvette or a winning lottery ticket. Instead, it means He will give us *new* desires, ones that will lead us closer to Him. We are incapable of generating a desire to love and serve God without His help, but when we ask, He gives us that desire.

> "WE ARE INCAPABLE OF GENERATING A DESIRE TO LOVE AND SERVE GOD WITHOUT HIS HELP, BUT WHEN WE ASK, HE GIVES US THAT DESIRE."

The longer we walk with the Lord, the more our desires change, usually without even realizing it. When my husband and I were first married we used to look forward to Thursday nights. We would throw together a simple dinner and then settle in for an evening of "must-see TV." Once we started a family, our schedule got busier and must-see TV evolved into "must get some sleep." Many years later I was flipping through the channels and landed on a rerun of one of our favorite shows from way back then. But now, I found I could hardly stand to watch it. The jokes were vulgar. The lifestyles of the characters were a mockery of the devastating results of sin that I had watched play out in the lives of real people. I was no longer entertained by it—on the contrary, it grieved me.

If someone had told me back then that it was not godly to watch that TV show, I would have smugly defended myself—claiming Christian freedom. I would resent the rule being placed on me and probably would have desired to watch it even more. Without realizing it, the Lord changed my desires. A supernatural change in desire is much more powerful to change behavior than the rules we give each other to require or forbid behavior.

As we live by the Spirit, we are no longer under the law—gritting our teeth while trying to obey a bunch of rules. When we abide in Christ, we will be supernaturally transformed over time and experience a greater desire to live in obedience to the Lord. We will be motivated by joy, not guilt. "This is love for God: to obey his commands. And his commands are not burdensome, for everyone born of God overcomes the world. This is the victory that has overcome the world, even our faith" (1 John 5:3–4).

Dependence

Although I hate to admit it, I have a big mouth. When I am not living by the Spirit, everyone knows it. I have learned that I need the Lord to temper my tongue so that I am useful to Him. Otherwise I can tear down the kingdom with that little member of my body. I depend on God, and, like the TV credit card commercial says, I have a "don't leave home without it" mentality. I often pray that the Lord would put a gate over my mouth and give me discretion not to say everything I think. I get into even more trouble when I try to be the center of attention or make people laugh. My weakness in this area is a good reminder that if I am not abiding in Christ, I can hurt others and wreak havoc with my tongue. It is not my desire to engage in such behavior but apart from abiding in Christ, this is who I become.

I am dependent upon the Lord to change me from the inside. In the South they have a saying: "Whatever is in the well comes up in the bucket." It's clearly a takeoff on Matthew 15:18, in which Jesus says: "But the things that come out of the mouth come from the heart, and these make a man 'unclean.'" Really, my mouth is not the problem at all—it's my heart that—when it is apart from Christ—is "unclean."

Abiding requires a constant awareness of how dependent we are upon the Lord. We learn to trust in His righteousness and not our own. We are utterly dependent upon Him to show us how to be useful, and being useful to the Lord becomes the believer's greatest joy. This also means depending upon Him in our relationships with others.

A friend of mine struggled for twenty years with unforgiveness toward her father, who had acted inappropriately with her as a child. She was a believer, but she didn't know how to forgive him (an unbeliever), even after reviewing all the verses about forgiveness in Scripture. Nowhere in scripture will you find steps on how to forgive. The reason is, you cannot do it. Christ must do it through you. I counseled my friend to ask Him to work this forgiveness in her heart and then wait for Him to do it.

She began to pray this way, and several months later the Lord provided her the opportunity to broach the subject with her father. After twenty years of not talking about the incident, her father broke down and asked her forgiveness. That resulted in a healing conversation. She extended her forgiveness and even shared the gospel with him. She did not have to figure out how to make it happen. She cried out to the Lord and He answered.

Colossians 3:12–17 lays out for us how we are to treat one another:

> Therefore, as God's chosen people, holy and dearly loved, clothe yourselves with compassion, kindness, humility, gentleness and patience. Bear with each other and forgive whatever grievances you may have against one another. Forgive as the Lord forgave you. And over all these virtues put on love, which binds them all together in perfect unity. Let the peace of Christ rule in your hearts, since as members of one body you were called to peace. And be thankful. Let the word of Christ dwell in you richly as you teach and admonish one another with all wisdom, and as you sing psalms, hymns and spiritual songs with gratitude in your hearts to God. And whatever you do, whether in word or deed, do it all in the name of the Lord Jesus, giving thanks to God the Father through him.

We are not able to accomplish a single one of these actions or attitudes in our own strength. To be able to live out these verses, we must depend on the power of the Spirit. Unfortunately, we often try to *be* the Holy Spirit for others—trying to control and motivate them with harsh words, coldness of heart, or with judgmental accusations.

I recall as a new convert that I began attending a Friday night Bible study. I was late each week because I had to shower before the study. I didn't want anyone to know that I was a smoker, one of the residuals of the party life I had left behind. Someone pulled me aside and confronted me that it wasn't honoring to the Lord for me to be late every week.

I remember thinking, *If you only knew how really sinful I am, you would think nothing of tardiness.* If that person had been filled with the Spirit and sought to really lead me into godly behavior, she would have approached me in a very different way. No one is motivated by guilt, so why do we keep using guilt on others (and even on ourselves)? Fortunately, I was so hungry and thirsty for truth that I didn't let that person keep me from coming to hear God's Word each week—late or not. In the weeks that followed, however, I avoided her out of fear that she would discover some of my more notable sins. She did not treat me with careful love but with self-righteous judgment.

Jesus and Women

Jesus has a different message for women than we have for each other—a message of mercy and grace. Look through the gospels at the narratives of His encounters with women: not once does He applaud a woman for her domestic skills. On several occasions, however, He commends women with great faith and reckless love. One word captures these women—humility. They approached Him needy and desperate, aware of their

> "LOOK THROUGH THE GOSPELS AT THE NARRATIVES OF HIS ENCOUNTERS WITH WOMEN: NOT ONCE DOES HE APPLAUD A WOMAN FOR HER DOMESTIC SKILLS."

unworthiness. He granted their requests for mercy. He welcomed their worship. Many of them became His close friends.

There is a third character present in most of the accounts of Jesus with women. This character takes different forms but is always the same—angry and judgmental. It may be a group of annoyed disciples begging Jesus to send away a nagging Canaanite woman, or a self-righteous Pharisee who thinks to himself, "*If this man were a prophet, he would know who is touching him and what kind of woman she is— that she is a sinner*" (Luke 7:39). On one occasion it was a crowd of bloodthirsty men with stones waiting to blame their brutality (against a woman caught in adultery) on Christ. There is even a sister, a fellow worshipper of Christ, tattling because her sister is not *doing* what is expected of her.

You know the story. Martha was busy serving and Mary was sitting at Jesus's feet. Often when this story is taught there is a disclaimer. It goes something like this: "Well, Mary should help her sister, but in this case she chose what was better" or "I'll tell you what, I'd rather stay at Martha's house." We feel for Martha. We've been where Martha has been. But that disclaimer never shows up in the Bible. This reveals our natural pull to focus on *doing* instead of *believing*. We secretly side with Martha and want to learn that later Mary helped her. But it's not there. Listen to what Jesus said: "Martha, Martha . . . you are worried and upset about many things, but *only one thing is needed*. Mary has chosen what is better, and it will not be taken away from her" (Luke 10:41–42, emphasis mine).

> "YET THE *ONE THING NEEDED* IS DRAWING NEAR TO CHRIST. THE REST OF OUR LIVES SHOULD FLOW FROM THAT ONE PURSUIT."

Anger is a natural reaction when the perception is a lack of respect for "the rules." Yet the *one thing needed* is drawing near to Christ. The rest of our lives should flow from that one pursuit. Martha ignored Christ to focus on things that didn't matter.

This is what we do too. I attended a women's event at my church. In fact, I headed up the committee that planned it. It was one of those events at which you go from one mini-seminar to another and then have lunch. These functions are meant to provide opportunity for fellowship and friendship to grow. In between seminars I found myself in a conversation about the gospel and realized I was speaking with someone who desperately needed to hear it. She and I stayed outside of the seminar. Five minutes later, someone poked her head out to warn me I was missing the talk on how to set a fabulous table. I assured her I would come in a minute. Five minutes later she poked her head out again: "Marci, you're missing it!" I wanted to say, "No, *you're* missing it!"

We get the gospel wrong all the time. Believers often think of it only for salvation of unbelievers. We rarely reflect on our own neediness for its power in daily life and miss the opportunities that come our way because we're so distracted with the externals. The true gospel sets women free to abandon man's ideal and draw near to Christ's. His standard is actually much higher than outward performance. It is inward devotion, desire, and dependence. Through freedom and grace received from Him, we are able to give freedom and grace to others rather than trying to control them. We are free to be emotional with Him (yes, you heard right). We are free to have transparent friendships, to dialogue without fear of judgment. When we admit weakness rather than covering it, we will be more useful to the kingdom than we've ever been.

In the Sermon on the Mount, Christ said, "Blessed are"—the poor in spirit, those who mourn, the meek, those who hunger and thirst for righteousness, the merciful, the pure in heart, the peacemakers, and those who are persecuted. Christ is describing people who are humble in heart, dependent, and needy. They are not self-righteous, thinking God is lucky to have them on His team. They know they are sinful. They know they have nothing to offer God but must receive everything from Him. They are in the right place to receive God's outrageous grace.

Making it Stick

- For discussion: *Abiding in Christ* is about understanding what it truly means to trust Christ with every aspect of your life. The Lord is working in each of us stirring desire, motivating devotion, and causing us to depend upon Him. How His work in us comes out in behavior will be different for each one of us depending on our personalities, our spiritual gifts, and our season of life. How can you know if you are abiding in Christ? What is your cue that you are not abiding (i.e., anger, fear, dissatisfaction, restlessness, a loss of peace)?

- The illustration of the devoted dog crying outside the closed door is an apt one to describe how we must seek Christ. Think about times you have cried out to God. How was the door opened? How does the psalmist cry out to God in Psalm 86? How is this similar to ways you have cried out to God? What truths about God does he recall for comfort?

5

A REAL ENEMY

I was saved in a large, high-profile church in southern California. The pastor there has come under a great deal of opposition from the local media over the years. False accusations, lawsuits, verbal and even physical attacks have been attempted to stop him from preaching the truth. These attacks have even come from people inside the church. There is a group of men there who have formed a "secret service" to protect the pastor—and the congregation, for that matter. These men recognize the dangers that lurk inside those four walls and are vigilant watchmen.

One Sunday, my husband and I settled into a pew eager to hear the message. A man with pink-tinted glasses came in and sat down in front of us, turned around, and stared at me. It was awkward and intrusive. I had compassion on him, thinking maybe he was mentally ill but I was also uncomfortable. I tried to ignore him and pretend I didn't notice. He did not stop staring even when the pastor began speaking, so I quietly said, "The pastor is up there." He turned to my husband and said "Let's go outside!" in a not-quite-human voice. I was immediately terrified. My husband's mouth dropped open and a man in a suit quietly slipped into the pew next to the man in the pink-tinted glasses. Within a few seconds, the man in the pink-tinted glasses got up and walked out. Then the man in the suit silently slipped out. A few minutes later we saw the man with the pink-tinted glasses walk in on the other side of the sanctuary and sit down on that side of the room. I prayed for whoever he sat near and for my heart to stop pounding.

To this day, I do not know what to make of that incident. I do know that neither I nor my husband heard the sermon that day. Everyone who was sitting around us witnessed it and talked with us about it afterward. "Man, I would've had your back if that guy caused any more trouble," one man said. "That was so weird," another piped in. We were all thinking the same thing but no one would say it. Even now I hate to suggest that the man was demon possessed. Unlike people in Jesus's day, we don't know what demon possession looks like in modern times.

Here's what I do know: The man in the pink-tinted glasses succeeded in distracting us from hearing the message that morning. I know that there is a real enemy of my soul out there in the spiritual realm. I know he is looking for ways to destroy my faith. He will use whatever means to do it. My only protection from his schemes is to abide in truth, and use the shield of faith to extinguish the enemy's lies (see Ephesians 6:16).

Denial Is Deadly

The Christian life is lived by faith. We never know what lies ahead, but we are warned in Scripture to be aware of the spiritual battle being waged, and to "put on the full armor of God" so that we can "take [our] stand against the devil's schemes" (Ephesians 6:11). We are armed with the knowledge that our "struggle is not against flesh and blood, but against the rulers, against the authorities, against the powers of this dark world and against the spiritual forces of evil in the heavenly realms" (Ephesians 6:12). The opposite of readiness is denial. Denial cordially invites the enemy to attack from behind. It is easy to fall into denial on many dangerous fronts. If we are not regularly reminding ourselves of God's truth, we *will* begin to believe lies—lies about God, lies about ourselves, lies that lead us to sin.

> "IF WE ARE NOT REGULARLY REMINDING OURSELVES OF GOD'S TRUTH, WE *WILL* BEGIN TO BELIEVE LIES."

Have you ever been walking on a dark night and felt that someone was following you? Your heart races, you walk faster, but you don't turn around. As the footsteps seem to get closer and faster you nearly break into a run, all the while telling yourself no one is there. Your senses scream danger but your mind tells you, *If I can't see it, it isn't real*. It refuses to face the truth.

Denial seems to be a common human response to danger. I took a self-defense class in college in which the instructor stressed to us that we must *never* be in denial about danger. He told us that if we sensed someone following us, we must turn and confidently face the potential perpetrator. The reasons he gave are:

1) A perpetrator looks for an unsuspecting person that he can attack from behind;
2) A perpetrator looks for someone who is alone and easily overtaken; and
3) A perpetrator looks for someone who is weak and fearful.

Denial can be deadly but seeing the truth can save your life. My instructor's first line of self-defense is designed to spoil the attacker's plan *before* he carries it out. Merely turning to face him eliminates all three things he is looking for in a victim. He will not catch you off-guard. He will not easily overtake you because you are able to see and assess the situation. By seeing clearly, you are better able to defend yourself and escape potential harm.

In the same way we convince ourselves no one is following us, we deny sin. Sin can blind anyone, even mature Christians. When we justify and deny sin, we are unable to identify it and repent of it—it gets us from behind. Just like Cain, our sin also crouches at the door waiting to master us (see Genesis 4:7). We will eventually act on whatever we entertain in our minds. If we don't see the danger in entertaining a temptation, then temptation will lead to sin, and sin gives birth to death (James 1:13–18). We think we can handle it. The longer we entertain it, the further entangled we become.

Amy suffered daily in a particularly painful marriage and learned to abide in Christ in her sadness and pain. We met together often and prayed regularly. Daily she brought the void of loneliness to the Lord to receive His comfort and found Him there—faithful to carry her. This was a difficult trial indeed. But no matter how closely she walked with the Lord, she was still brokenhearted over her loveless union.

The enemy saw Amy's hardship as an opportunity to strike from behind. He capitalized on her felt needs and patiently built a trap that would lead her astray in almost undetectable steps. Most women have a God-given desire for male companionship. Women in painful marriages, however, need to be careful because they are easily tempted to fulfill their God-given desire for male companionship in an inappropriate and sinful way.

Amy met a man who was kind to her and they became friends. These things almost never begin (for a woman anyway) as a sexual allurement. She enjoyed the friendship and the kindness he extended her. He filled a void that was left by her husband's coldness. She began justifying excessive time on the phone with him and their relationship grew into something more than friendship. After months of believing little lies about the innocence of this friendship, Amy fell headlong into denial. Even though she knew it was wrong, she began to entertain the idea of leaving her husband to start over again with this new man. *Surely God wants me to be happy*, she told herself. This man promised to take care of her and love her and planned to leave his wife as well. In the midst of being carried away and enticed, she admitted her feelings to me.

From the outside looking in, I knew it was a trap and she was being enticed by some very dangerous bait. I urged her to repent, turn to the Lord, and shed light on the situation before she gave in to his physical advances. Once she turned to face her attacker (Satan) and realized what was happening through the lens of scripture, she was able to see it clearly for what it was and ended the relationship. Over time as this other man's true colors were revealed, she was relieved that the Lord rescued her before she had acted on the sin she had been entertaining in her mind.

> "WE MUST NOT BE IN DENIAL ABOUT OUR TENDENCY TOWARD SIN, OUR ABILITY TO RESIST IT, OR THE EXISTENCE OF SATAN."

We must not be in denial about our tendency toward sin, our ability to resist it, or the existence of Satan, our tempter. Denying his existence or his influence is what allows him to attack from behind. He is real, although he would like us to believe that he is not. Amy confessed her sin to her pastor and eventually her husband. Exposing sin and confessing it robs it of power and causes the enemy to flee. A physical enemy may desire to rob us of our possessions or take our life, but our spiritual enemy is out to destroy our *faith*. Faith depends on truth. If Satan can get us to believe lies, he has succeeded in his malefaction, for belief leads to behavior.

Fighting Lies with Truth

Satan is looking for the same thing the perpetrator mentioned above is looking for—an easy target. Being aware of him and his tactics is the first line of defense against him. 1 Peter 5:8 warns that our "enemy the devil prowls around like a roaring lion looking for someone to devour." He will use whatever means possible to attack us. Our protection is found through the shield of faith "with which you can extinguish all the flaming arrows of the evil one" (Ephesians 6:16).

> "SATAN IS LOOKING FOR AN EASY TARGET."

I have struggled with nightmares for years. I don't know if it is because I am a visual person (even if I see a frightening movie trailer it will visit me in my dreams) or because I eat too close to bedtime. Once I watched a movie about dinosaurs that didn't scare me in the theater. But for six months afterward, I had terrifying nightmares about me and my loved ones being chased and eaten by dinosaurs.

As I have grown in my knowledge and love for Christ, my nightmares have not been as frequent but I still occasionally wake up in a cold sweat. There are times when I feel like the perpetrator from my nightmare is standing right there in the room lurking in the shadows. I have to fight fear with a conscious effort to believe God's truth. I know that no one can harm me apart from God's permission. I know that I will not go through anything that He will not also give me the strength to go through. I speak these things to myself, *not* to the presence in my room. I pray for protection. Eventually the truth calms me down and I am able to finish my night of sleep.

All that we know about the spiritual realm is what God has revealed in His Word. We are not told to seek out the enemy, talk to him, challenge him, or even rebuke him. We know that "the one who is in you is greater than the one who is in the world" (1 John 4:4). With that knowledge, as we encounter frightening situations, we are to run to our Father, put on the holy armor He has given us, and cling to what we know to be true.

Lies, Lies, and More Lies

Revelation 12:9 calls Satan: "the great dragon . . . the ancient serpent called the devil" who "leads the whole world astray." Some of his lies are overt. Some are subtle. Consciously believing truth instead of his lies is the only thing that causes him to flee.

Asaph spent many sleepless nights tossing and turning with anxiety. He was tempted to believe the enemy's lies when he was in a season of distress and God seemed far away:

> I cried out to God for help;
> I cried out to God to hear me.
> When I was in distress, I sought the Lord;
> at night I stretched out untiring hands
> and my soul refused to be comforted.
> I remembered you, O God, and I groaned;
> I mused, and my spirit grew faint.
>   Selah

> You kept my eyes from closing;
> I was too troubled to speak.
> I thought about the former days,
> the years of long ago;
> I remembered my songs in the night.
> My heart mused and my spirit inquired:
> Will the Lord reject forever?
> Will he never show his favor again?
> Has his unfailing love vanished forever?
> Has his promise failed for all time?
> Has God forgotten to be merciful?
> Has he in anger withheld his compassion?
>   Selah (Psalm 77:1–9)

He didn't have the luxury of popping a sleeping pill and slipping peacefully into denial. In order to combat these lies the psalmist worked it out by rehearsing the things he knew to be true about God.

> To this I will appeal:
> the years of the right hand of the Most High."
> I will remember the deeds of the LORD;
> yes, I will remember your miracles of long ago.
> I will meditate on all your works
> and consider all your mighty deeds.
> Your ways, O God, are holy.
> What god is as great as our God?
> You are the God who performs miracles;
> you display your power among the peoples. (Psalm 77:10–14)

His spirit lifted as he worked through present difficulties by remembering God's faithfulness in the past. We can comfort ourselves by remembering all that God has brought us through. This is how our faith grows and how we can rest in His faithfulness for the future.

We Were Not Made to Be Islands

God does not help those who help themselves. He helps those who *cannot* help themselves. This is proven true over and over in the Bible. This week, while writing on this subject, I have been wrestling with worry over a friend of mine who has escaped an abusive relationship. She was saved out of a hopeless existence and has found

> "GOD DOES NOT HELP THOSE WHO HELP THEMSELVES. HE HELPS THOSE WHO *CANNOT* HELP THEMSELVES."

great joy in the freedom of the gospel but quickly gives in to fear and the feeling she should be "doing" something.

She hadn't returned my calls or e-mails for several weeks and I began to despair, knowing what lies she was probably believing in the absence of any fellowship with believers. Her abuser had tried to kill her twice but she was still drawn to him. I felt helpless and started to feel like I should be doing something. My prayers for her have been urgent. Not coincidentally, she finally called me this week. She was embarrassed to call because she had fallen into such a depression that she actually tried to take her own life and had spent some time in the hospital. As I listened to her, the lies she had been believing came tumbling out. "Marci, the harder I try, it seems the worse things get. I try to be honest and do right but bad things keep happening. I probably need some counseling or something. I can't figure out what's wrong with me."

I didn't deny that some Biblical counseling would be a good idea. I told her: "Yes, get some counseling, but in the meantime let me go ahead and diagnose your problem. You isolated yourself from the body of Christ. As soon as you did that, the enemy came in with his old tricks of fear and striving." I started filling her mind with *truth*. I reminded her that when she was in the fellowship and being taught truth, how joyful she was and how clear her objectives in life became. How she trusted in the Lord with all her heart and He did indeed direct her path (Proverbs 3:5–6). The Lord opened doors for a new job and even laid it on a dentist's heart to replace some teeth that her abuser had knocked out. It was only when she decided that she "got it from here, Lord" that things starting getting out of control. I told her I knew she was believing those lies because they are the same lies I believe when I isolate myself from the body of Christ.

Even Peter believed that he was strong enough to stand against temptation. He believed a lie about his own strength when he said, "Lord, I am ready to go with you to prison and to death." Jesus answered, "I tell you, Peter, before the rooster crows today, you will deny three times that you know me" (Luke 22:33–34). After his fall, Peter was fully aware of his weakness and where he needed to get the power to stand firm. He had experienced the power of Satan and discovered what it took to resist him.

To live in the Lord's strength means to believe His Word and act accordingly. It's another way of describing what it means to abide in Christ. My daughter and I recently had a conversation about how the enemy lies to us today. I asked her if she thought that Eve regretted eating the forbidden fruit in the garden. She thought about it for a minute and then replied, "I bet she regretted that every day of her life."

A Real Enemy

Eve believed the enemy's lies and no doubt did wish that she could go back and undo that moment. Think how often today's teenagers are tempted to engage in premarital sex. The enemy, using the form of a handsome young man or a sweet young woman, will promise love, rapturous joy, and commitment. In a weak moment it seems so appealing and "feels right," but those feelings quickly change to feelings of being used, alone, and shamed. The consequences have made many young people wish they could go back and undo what cannot be undone.

We cannot blame Satan for all the evil in our lives. We are weak and prone to fall to our sinful desires. James 1:14 says, "Each one is tempted when, by his *own* evil desire, he is dragged away and enticed" (emphasis mine). A mouse is so attracted to a piece of cheese that he doesn't see the dangerous platform it sits on. In the same way our flesh can be drawn in by some allurement but blind to the consequences. Only true believers have the power to resist the devil—but even we can fall into his traps.

The point is, we are all weak. Satan is a worthy foe. Anyone who thinks she can resist the enemy in her own strength is a fool. There is safety in numbers. The body of Christ is a safety net against the sin that so easily entangles us. Being present in the body of Christ is essential to avoiding the enemy's traps. It is where we are regularly encouraged to run to the One who is greater than our enemy—for protection, the strength to stand firm in faith, and the reminder of the joyful freedom that comes from abiding in Christ.

Making it Stick

- Remember that the devil is like a mugger: he will attack from behind, he is looking for someone who is alone

Super(free)Woman

and thus easily overpowered, someone who is self-righteous and therefore caught unaware, or someone whose faith is already weak due to personal tribulation and fear. Can you think of a time in your life that these circumstances were present? What happened? Do you think you are still an easy target?

- Read Luke 22:24–34. What argument arose among the disciples that preceded Jesus's exclamation to Peter in verses 31 and 32? What did Jesus pray for Peter?

- Think about it: Nowhere in the Bible does it say God helps those who help themselves! In fact, God helps those who *cannot* help themselves. How does this make you feel about all the time you spend trying to "stay on top of things"?

6

STANDING FIRM

As God's word has penetrated my heart, counseling others has become simpler—not easier, necessarily, but much less confusing. I am learning to quickly identify what lies people have been clinging to. Usually, it is disillusionment with something they thought would make them happy. Once the lies are exposed and compared to Scripture, it becomes only a matter of training individuals to use the shield of faith to combat the lies. To live by faith is to abide in Christ. It is more powerful than anything I have ever witnessed in counseling situations. I have had the joy of a front-row seat watching God's truth defeat everything from depression to OCD to chronic anxiety disorder—even extreme anorexia and self-mutilation.

Satan and his fallen angels study us, find our weaknesses, and attack us in those vulnerable places. When they succeed in making us fall, then they accuse us of failure. Their first line of attack is on our minds. They lie to us, accuse us, and plant seeds of fear, guilt, and shame. They convince us we must take control of our circumstances instead of trusting God through them. We learn about Satan's schemes and how to stand firm against him as we read about the spiritual battle we face every day in Ephesians chapter 6.

Being aware that there is a spiritual war is the first line of defense.

> "BEING AWARE THAT THERE IS A SPIRITUAL WAR IS THE FIRST LINE OF DEFENSE."

In times of war, the intelligence division is essential. Understanding how the enemy operates makes us more successful in thwarting his plan (see 2 Corinthians 2:11). If Satan's one objective is to get you to fall—then your one objective is to stand.

A young girl I met with was saved out of a world of sin. She had been heavily involved in drugs, drinking, and promiscuity. She was grateful to be saved and set free from her bondage to wickedness but was still drawn to one particular individual from her past. He was her first love—if you could call it that. Years before she had lost her virginity to him in what could amount to date rape. Nonetheless, he had a hold on her. They had an on-again, off-again relationship. When she came to Christ it had been off for a while. Sure enough, only a few short weeks into her newfound faith, guess who showed up on her doorstep?

She invited him in, believing she was strong enough in her faith to witness to him. Maybe the Lord would save him and they could be happy together in a new context. It was a trap she did not see coming. She was alone and caught off guard. She was too weak to resist his advances. She gave in to temptation and he stayed with her all weekend. For weeks afterward, she was tormented by guilt and accusations from the enemy: You will never be a Christian! Look how weak you are! The Lord does not want you now! What if someone at church finds out? You might as well go back to your old life—that is *who* you are. She did end the relationship for good but like many new believers, instead of repenting and believing Christ died for that sin, she tried to forget it, work harder, and do more Christian things to offset the guilt.

So often, Christians try to fight the enemy with religious activity. Yet the Bible does not recommend activity as a solution to our problems. It says when (not if) the day of evil comes, put on the armor and stand firm. All of these pieces of armor were issued to us at the moment of salvation and are applied by faith (His truth, His righteousness, readiness that comes from His gospel, His salvation, His Spirit). The only action a Christian contributes is faith (if you can call that an action). The Philippian jailer asked Paul, "What must I *do* to be saved?" (Acts 16:30). Paul answered, "*Believe* in the Lord Jesus, and you will be saved" (Acts 16:31).

> "SO OFTEN, CHRISTIANS TRY TO FIGHT THE ENEMY WITH RELIGIOUS ACTIVITY."

Many Christians believe it is God's grace that saved them, but they also believe the lie that says they must do or be "good" to remain in His favor. They don't understand that they have inherited *His* righteousness (Romans 3:21–22). No one can be good apart from regular communication with the Lord. We fall short in our attempts to be good because it is the power of His Word that changes us, not our own ability. As we grow in knowledge and love for the Savior, our behavior will begin to change. In his book *Abide in Christ* (Whitaker House, 1979), Andrew Murray points out the error of those who don't understand that weakness and failure are actually the conduits of abiding.

Super(free)Woman

The idea they have of grace is this: that their conversion and pardon are God's work but that now, in gratitude to God, it is their work to live as Christians and follow Jesus. There is always the thought of a work that has to be done, and even though they pray for help, still the work is theirs. They fail continually and become hopeless, and the despondency only increases the helplessness. No, wandering one; as it was Jesus who drew you when He spoke, "Come" (Matthew 11:28), so it is Jesus who keeps you when He said, "Abide" (John 15:4). The grace to come and the grace to abide alike are from Him alone.

Suffering and failure reveal who we are and who we put our trust in—ourselves or God. They show us our need for God when we have exhausted all of our human effort and wisdom. It is still painful to go through trials even when trusting God through them. But there is peace in the knowledge that: "after you have suffered a little while, [God] will himself restore you and make you strong, firm and steadfast" (1 Peter 5:10).

Eliphaz, Bildad, and Zophar Got It Wrong!

People suffer. Satan loves to add guilt to grief as unwanted advice flows from the mouths of well-meaning people. We learn what *not* to do from Job's friends. The Lord said to Eliphaz: "I am angry with you and your two friends, because you have not spoken of me what is right, as my servant Job has" (Job 42:7). Platitudes spoken to someone in pain are as unwelcome and awkward as an uninvited drunk at

> "PLATITUDES SPOKEN TO SOMEONE IN PAIN ARE AS UNWELCOME AND AWKWARD AS AN UNINVITED DRUNK AT A PARTY."

a party. Assumptions are painful to bear. Requiring a suffering person to follow rules for "suffering well" is not only anti-gospel, it is cruel. The body of Christ was meant to comfort the suffering believer—but sometimes they get it wrong. *[margin note: so, what do you do? Serve them silently?]*

The wife of a youth pastor carried her baby full term, safely delivered and enjoyed snuggling him for one day. The next day, speeding to the hospital, he breathed his last, leaving her to reconcile how this could be happening. She reached out to the church. The leadership officially informed her that she must joyfully accept this as God's will for her life. Then they handed her a gift certificate for a free turkey.

The day after the funeral, the women's ministry leaders met. It was business as usual, checking items off the agenda. She was present in body only. She could feel her body preparing to feed a baby that was no longer in her arms. Her thoughts went back to the day prior. As she had laid her hand on his tiny casket, all she could think about was the gaze of those around her—those who would hold her accountable to keep her emotions in check. Over the next few months, people showed up—not with food, gifts, or encouragement—but with exhortation. She need not spend her days mourning. That would not be pleasing to the Lord, they said. She dutifully held back her tears, believing the lie that the Lord would be displeased if she shed even one.

Thirteen years later, the tears flowed freely as she recounted these events to me. I could not imagine where this teaching came from or who would have the audacity to enforce it. Jesus did not forbid grief. He never turned away a woman for being emotional. He Himself wept on several occasions—most notably at Lazarus' tomb. Coldness is never appropriate in the body of Christ. It

> "JESUS DID NOT FORBID GRIEF. HE NEVER TURNED AWAY A WOMAN FOR BEING EMOTIONAL."

will not motivate anyone to Christ-like behavior. The lie that purports joyful suffering as keeping a stiff upper lip and a painted-on smile adds hundreds of pounds to the burden suffering people are already carrying. Joyful suffering is based on knowledge that someday God will wipe every tear away. Until then, joy and tears often go together.

Divide and Conquer

Suffering softens some hearts and hardens others. Satan loves to convince us that we are the only unhappy person in the room. When people believe the lie that they are suffering from a hardship that no one else has, they feel entitled to retreat, to stay away from their church family until they can put on a mask of happiness and force a smile. They believe they can't serve the body of Christ because they have nothing to offer. This is the exact opposite response a Christian should have. When we are suffering, we need the body of Christ more than ever—but our enemy wants to get us alone. That is where he can successfully lie to us. He gets us to believe that his thoughts are our thoughts. We can easily misperceive reality when we're alone. My pastor always says, "You are your own worst counselor." He's right. We need each other.

Sitting in a restaurant one afternoon I was eating lunch with two ladies. One of them was my good friend and the other was a new acquaintance. The latter began openly sharing her discontentedness with her marriage. I had compassion on her. Her disappointment was evident. To my surprise she began comparing her unhappy marriage with my seemingly happy marriage. I asked her how she knew I had a happy marriage. She stated some assumptions based on her perceptions from what we looked like on Sunday mornings. I told her that I had my share of struggles in marriage but she dismissed them as small and unimportant based on what she had observed.

Undeterred, she then continued to compare her marriage with that of the other woman present. My eyes met my friend's and then dropped to my salad. Unbeknownst to the woman who was speaking, just two years prior, I had counseled this very friend through a severe crisis in her marriage. She had found great freedom and victory on the other side of that painful trial. Neither of us would dishonor our husbands in order to correct this woman's wrong assumptions.

She assumed we did not understand her pain and therefore could not judge the actions she planned to take. In her mind we could not present her with truth because we could not understand the depth of the temptation. She believed the lie that her marriage was beyond repair and that she was the only one who suffered this way. She was so focused on escaping her suffering that she could not see what good things could have come from it. She was determined to "take over from here." I did not see her much after that lunch. She eventually disappeared from our fellowship. Once we isolate ourselves, the enemy will be right there to overtake us with lies we willingly believe.

Whether or not we can understand someone else's struggles, we all understand temptation. James is very clear when he describes temptation in hunting terms. We are enticed by bait. As soon as we grab hold of it we are dragged away to our death, like an animal caught in a trap. The woman at lunch was eyeing some bait that both my friend and I had also been tempted by in one form or another. She was weak and unwilling to resist the enemy's lies. My friend and I tried to warn her that it was a trap but she was blinded by the bait.

Where's My Happily Ever After?

One of Satan's most successful schemes is to convince us that there is something or someone who will bring us our "happily ever after" here on earth. C. S. Lewis put it this way in his book *Mere Christianity*: "If I find within myself a desire which no experience in this world can satisfy, then the most probable explanation is that I was made for another world."

No person or material thing has ever brought us lasting happiness, so why do we continue to believe the lie that something or someone will? The whole of creation is groaning under the curse that leads to this frustrating search for ultimate satisfaction—especially believers.

> "NO PERSON OR MATERIAL THING HAS EVER BROUGHT US LASTING HAPPINESS, SO WHY DO WE CONTINUE TO BELIEVE THE LIE THAT SOMETHING OR SOMEONE WILL?"

Not only so, but we ourselves, who have the firstfruits of the Spirit, groan inwardly as we wait eagerly for our adoption as sons, the redemption of our bodies. For in this hope we were saved. But hope that is seen is no hope at all. Who hopes for what he already has? But if we hope for what we do not yet have, we wait for it patiently (Romans 8:23-25).

Many women seem to have an unwritten list of things they think will make them happy. Walt Disney told us that once Prince Charming came along, we would live happily ever after. Many of us believed him. So after marriage, a baby was usually next on the list. Perhaps attaining money, living in a beautifully decorated home, wearing designer clothes, or having

> "WHATEVER WE THINK WILL MAKE US HAPPY, APART FROM CHRIST, IS A LIE."

friends in certain social circles became part of that happiness list. Every woman's list would be somewhat different but also very much alike. But whatever we think will make us happy—apart from Christ—is a lie. It is idolatry. Any one of these things can bring temporary joy, but when they become our number-one pursuit, they become idols that bring disappointment and disillusionment. The disappointment we experience with being unable to live happily ever after is meant to fuel our hope for eternity.

Although the ultimate spiritual war has been won at the cross, we still face daily battles while we wait for our eternal rescue. The armor of the Lord girds our minds and hearts, allowing us to thwart our adversary with the only offensive weapon we have, "the sword of the Spirit, which is the word of God" (Ephesians 6:17). Jesus Himself used scripture to fight off the temptations of the enemy. There is only one way to be transformed from believing lies to believing truth. Romans 12:2 says we are transformed by the renewing of our minds. That means we need to get the word of God in our heads in whatever way we can. We can't believe it or abide in it if we don't know what it says.

As a young mother of two active children it was difficult for me to sit down and read anything. I would fall asleep within minutes from exhaustion. I became dependent on Bible teachers on the radio to feed me scriptural truths. I learned to plan my day around my favorite teachers—fold laundry at ten thirty, clean house at two o'clock. These teachers, along with my pastor on Sunday mornings, spoke truth into my life so my mind wouldn't be idle and therefore entertain lies. After all, it is hard to believe

"NONE OF THE BIBLICAL WRITERS LAID OUT A BIBLE-READING PLAN OR MEMORIZATION SCHEDULE."

the Lord will use you for anything when you spend all day washing clothes and cleaning up toys. But His truth stored up in my heart during those years.

None of the biblical writers laid out a Bible-reading plan or memorization schedule or formulas for prayer. The reason is that spiritual disciplines will play out very differently for different people in different stages of life. Instead the biblical writers call us to a higher standard than merely a disciplined life: to love His Word, believe it, hide it in our hearts, and to pray without ceasing.

The Power of Prayer

Once each month a group of women from my church conduct a chapel service at a mission for recovering addicts, also women. After many years of doing this, our program is well organized. It is easy to put our faith in our well-run program and forget the true source of our power. Over the course of a few months recently, we recognized hardness in the hearts of many of those we ministered to. This makes it difficult to communicate and build relationships with them.

One of the newer women from our church, Lydia, confided in me that she felt guilty going with us because she wanted to come and hear the teaching and enjoy the fellowship, but she didn't feel she had anything to offer. She said she was intimidated by the rough lifestyles of the mission women. Being convicted about her feelings, Lydia committed herself to pray for one of the women at the mission every day. She did this without telling anyone.

The next month we faced the same disappointing hardness of heart in everyone—except one woman. Lydia sat next to the woman she had been praying for and simply asked her, "How are you?" Without knowing Lydia had prayed for her all month, the woman began to open up. Lydia gave her some simple counsel, prayed with her, and found herself overjoyed at how God used her even though she felt she was weak. The newest believer among us shamed us all by her childlike faith and her willingness to be used through prayer.

> "IF YOU DON'T PRAY, IT IS NOT BECAUSE YOU ARE NOT DISCIPLINED ENOUGH. IT IS BECAUSE YOU DON'T REALLY *BELIEVE* IN THE POWER OF IT."

The truth is if we believed in the power of prayer we would do it. If you don't pray, it is not because you are not disciplined enough. It is because you don't really *believe* in the power of it. We prove that we believe more in our human ingenuity by our prayerless lives. In the same way a human relationship grows closer by time spent together communicating—so does our relationship with God. He is not as concerned with how or when we pray as much as He is with whether or not we *pray*. We don't have to worry about our prayers being eloquent or modeled after someone else. "The Spirit helps us in our weakness. We do not know what we ought to pray for, but the Spirit himself intercedes for us with groans that words cannot express" (Romans 8:26).

We may be overwhelmed at the thought of fighting a war (especially with an unseen enemy) until we realize over and over we are merely called to stand. Actively believing the truth protects us from falling. Our behavior will follow our belief. When the dust clears and we look up, we will see that Christ fought the war for us. All we did was believe Him. It is our faith that shields us from the enemy's fiery darts.

Making it Stick

- Think about how the enemy trips you up: Does he keep you busy with unimportant things causing you to disregard your priorities? Are you a perfectionist? If you don't have time for the "perfect quiet time" do you just avoid spending any time with the Lord? Has Satan deceived you into believing in a "happily ever after" here on earth? Do you think that there is someone or something that you don't have now that would bring you satisfaction if you could just attain it? Does Satan successfully attack you in the same way every time? Do you get upset—like I do—when you realize you've been an easy target? The Lord is calling each of us to put on His armor and to *stand firm*.

- We women tend to hold ourselves to high standards of behavior; our mothers may have taught us to "put on a happy face." And sometimes this is good advice: petty complaints take on lives of their own when we focus on them. But in times of sorrow, in particular, keeping a stiff upper lip seems unbearable. Even Jesus wept. Think about how to be authentic about grief—your own and others'. The apostle Paul did not hide his grief. Read 2 Corinthians 1:3–11 and observe his openness about how he "despaired even of life." What good things came out of it (vv. 4, 6, 9–11)?

7

A POWERFULLY MUNDANE LIFE

Brother Lawrence, a seventeenth-century monk, was clumsy and crippled from a war injury and admitted he could not do anything well. He worked for the first half of his adult life in the kitchen of a monastery and the second half in the sandal shop. His daily life was consumed with washing dishes and fixing other men's used sandals. He died unaware of the impact his life would have on thousands of people—even several hundred years later.

During his life he wrote letters to friends explaining the joy he and others had in their relationship with Christ. To one friend he wrote: "I am taking this opportunity to tell you about the sentiments of one of our society concerning the admirable effects and continual assistance he receives from the presence of God . . . For the past forty years his continual care has been to be always with God . . . He is now so accustomed to that divine presence that he receives from God continual comfort and peace . . . his soul has been filled with joy and delight so continual, and sometimes so great, that he is forced to find ways to hide their appearing outwardly to others who may not understand." He found that being mindful of the Lord's presence and thinking about the truth of Scripture—even during the busiest times of the day—came with supernatural peace and joy.

Brother Lawrence's small circle of friends was so impacted by his life and testimony that they felt he had a secret that needed to be shared with the world. They got together after his death, compiled their letters from him, and had them published. The end result was a little book called *The Practice of the Presence of God*. The following is an excerpt:

> God has many ways of drawing us to Himself. He sometimes seems to hide Himself from us. But faith alone ought to be our support. Faith is the foundation of our confidence. We must put all our faith in God. He will not fail us in time of need. I do not know how God will dispose of me, but I am always happy. All the world suffers and I, who deserve the severest discipline, feel joys so continual and great that I can scarcely contain them. I would willingly ask God for a part of your sufferings.
>
> I know my weakness is so great that, if He left me one moment to myself, I would be the most wretched man alive. Yet, I do not know how He could leave me alone because faith gives me as strong a conviction as reason. He never forsakes us until we have first forsaken Him. Let us fear to leave Him. Let us always be with Him. Let us live and die in His presence. Do pray for me, and I pray for you.

What Brother Lawrence discovered was no secret—it was the power of abiding in faith. He experienced the mighty power of the gospel through his weakness. He did not take on the establishment like Martin Luther, his predecessor who lived in the late fifteenth and early sixteenth centuries. He simply understood his weakness and believed in the sufficiency of God's grace and forgiveness. This man, who spent his life as a common worker, impacted the world simply by abiding in Christ and doing what was right in front of him to do.

Over the years I have observed Christians immerse themselves in all sorts of causes. During my childhood I remember many Christians signing up to sell products through a multilevel marketing company—they all became very passionate about soap. Even good causes can distract us from the gospel; politics, the environment, public health issues, homeschooling, vegetarian eating (or any other kind of special diet), exercise—the list is endless. While many of these issues have redeeming qualities, Christians are not commanded or forbidden in Scripture to participate in them. If we do participate, we are not to put our faith in them or allow them to take center stage in our lives. Often Christians will use scripture verses to back these sorts of things up, but these external things do not draw us near to God (1 Corinthians 8:8).

> "WHEN CHRISTIANS GET DISTRACTED WITH "GOOD THINGS" THEY OFTEN END UP LOSING THEIR PASSION FOR THE GOSPEL."

When Christians get distracted with "good things" they often end up losing their passion for the gospel—which is the power of God unto salvation (Romans 1:16). I have a relative who became so passionate about homeopathic healing that she talked about it with everyone she encountered. She used to be that bold with the gospel. All of her energy turned from rescuing people's souls to rescuing their temporal bodies.

Guilt or Grace

Years ago my husband and I started listening to a popular financial planner heard daily on the radio. He has a lot of good ideas but we found that if we listen to him for very long we become obsessed with getting out of debt and building a large savings for our children to inherit. That is a good thing but it is not the gospel. We could spend all our time building a financial legacy for our children and never spend time with our children in order to invest in what we really desire to leave behind—the gospel of Jesus Christ. Hebrews 13:9 says, "It is good for our hearts to be strengthened by grace." Often we are more motivated by guilt than we are by grace.

I have observed that most sermons have one of two objectives: 1) to motivate people with guilt to *do* something, or 2) to motivate people with truth to *believe* something. Every preacher desires to motivate his audience. Guilt is a powerful tool that motivates behavior—short term. Truth is an even more powerful tool that motivates belief, which then motivates behavior—long term. Jesus offers to take away our guilt, setting us free from its bondage. The hardest part is admitting our guilt and *believing* He will take it away. Instead we try to cover it and vow to *do* better next time.

I received a call from a woman in the church one Sunday afternoon. She was wrestling with some of the same struggles I had early in my Christian walk, and was seeking some accountability. She asked if I would meet with her regularly to make sure she was doing what she should be doing to avoid falling back into old patterns. She is fortunate she did not initiate this conversation with me a few years ago. I might have set up weekly meetings and given her a checklist of duties to monitor her growth. How arrogant of me to think I could control someone else's spiritual growth with rules! I can't even discipline myself.

Instead, I told her I had a joyful message for her. We set a time to meet for coffee. The next day, with Starbucks in hand, I explained that we all fear falling back into old patterns. Our human tendency is to find a tangible priest, put laws in place, and vow to never allow this. But trying to mesh Alcoholics Anonymous rules with the gospel doesn't work. I don't have the power to keep her from falling. I could only speak truth to her. After being saved supernaturally by the grace of our Lord Jesus Christ, do we doubt His ability to finish the job? Must we take over from here?

> "AFTER BEING SAVED SUPERNATURALLY BY THE GRACE OF OUR LORD JESUS CHRIST, DO WE DOUBT HIS ABILITY TO FINISH THE JOB?"

Again, the gospel comes to our rescue, freeing us from these entanglements. We remember to believe in the power of Jesus to transform us—not in ourselves or any other human agent. "He who began a good work in you will carry it on to completion until the day of Christ Jesus" (Philippians 1:6). The Bible reminds us our dependence is on Him.

Having said this, the Lord does use friendship in our spiritual growth. Our friends tend to see the blind spots we miss. Accountability happens naturally as trust and love are established between two people. Confrontations are effective when delivered in love and humility, in the context of privacy and trust. This is why the book of Hebrews exhorts believers not to forsake the fellowship. As we live our lives, regularly rubbing shoulders in the body of Christ, we have conversations with many friends. We hear biblical teaching. We share prayer requests. We encourage each other with scripture, recognizing that we are all prone to wander.

I encouraged my new friend to let our relationship (and others) develop naturally. I warned her not to put her faith in me or any other "mentor" but to cling instead to Christ. Due to the similarity of our struggles, we could warn each other of the dangers of believing Satan's lies. We could remind each other about finding strength in the truth of God's Word. We could pray for each other. We could encourage others in the church to engage in friendships, and ultimately, true fellowship, like this. And, although we realize that our struggle is not yet over, we can hope together in the time when it will be.

All true believers will someday stand shoulder to shoulder at the throne of grace. In that day, we will see how weak and prideful we were on this earth. No one will foolishly compare herself to the person standing next to her. No one will gather followers to himself. We will be too consumed with Christ. In that day, we will all marvel at His grace and wonder that He saved such wretched, sinful, undeserving people like us.

What's Your Something?

What does it mean to live by faith and not by sight in practical terms (2 Corinthians 5:7)? We were all born with an instinctive desire to put our faith in something that we believe will bring satisfaction. All our hopes and dreams are centered on that something. When sin entered the scene in Genesis chapter 3, mankind abandoned pursuit of God and instead pursued the desires of the flesh. If we were honest with ourselves, even believers would have to admit that our "something" is not always God. Our earthly "somethings" often change as one by one they turn out to be disappointing.

To live by faith means our "something" is Christ. To live by faith means we believe that He Himself is our reward—not what He can give us (Genesis 15:1). Like He did with Abraham, God reveals Himself to us. Our job is to believe Him. "Abraham believed the LORD, and he credited it to him as righteousness" (Genesis 15:6).

If we are truthful with ourselves we will find that most of the things we want to put our faith in are tangible (marriage, job, children, friendship, health, money, status). Many of these are "good things" but they will never satisfy our deepest longings. They are not our ultimate reward.

> "OUR THOUGHTS MOTIVATE OUR ACTIVITIES."

Whatever our "something" is, it can become an idol that consumes our thoughts. Our thoughts motivate our activities. If our "something" is money, then our thoughts will revolve around creative ways to make it, spend it, invest it, and so on. If it is marriage or children, then we may conduct our relationships according to what we believe works, rather than how God says to conduct them. Even religious activity can become an idol if pursued for selfish reasons—maybe to please people or gain recognition.

We like formulas and guarantees: if I do X, then I will receive Y. We like to feel that we are in control of our own happiness. I have sat with many disillusioned women who have fallen into the trap of entitlement. They believe that if they behave a certain way, then God owes them earthly blessing. They tell me they have done everything right and cannot understand why they haven't received their blessing from God. This attitude is prideful and displays a misunderstanding of God's grace. "What then shall we say that Abraham, our forefather, discovered in this matter? If, in fact, Abraham was justified by works, he had something to boast about—but not before God . . . Now when a man works, his wages are not credited to him as a gift, but as an obligation. However, to the man who does not work but trusts God who justifies the wicked, his faith is credited as righteousness" (Romans 4:1–2, 4–5).

God does not negotiate. He won't be manipulated into giving us what we want by our seemingly good behavior. He owes no one. Everything He does is for our good and His glory—even if it doesn't *feel* good.

Red Spots

I woke up one morning in May 2006 to find my hands covered in red spots. My first thought was that I'd had an allergic reaction to some lotion or soap because the rash ended abruptly at my wrist. I wasn't concerned. When I pulled the covers back, swung my feet out of bed and leaned over to my first steps of the day, a tide of fear swept over me. Red spots also covered my feet, ending abruptly at my ankles.

Like many people—and I don't know why we do—I went into denial. Surely it was just a freak allergy and nothing to worry about. I let it go until I could not ignore it any longer. The rash began to morph. The red spots turned into purple welts and spread to meet each other. I knew I had to take action when a store clerk looked at the money I was handing her, recoiled with a little gasp, and looked at me like I was a leper.

Over the course of the next few months I was given test after test by a variety of doctors. At any given time I had a Band-aid with a big piece of cotton under it somewhere on my body. The word *lupus* was thrown around more than any other. One doctor said, "I'm sure you have lupus but don't go home and google it." So the first thing I did when I got home was google it! Another seed of fear took root as I looked at pictures of worst-case scenarios and read about impending kidney failure. I turned my computer off, realizing I should have obeyed my doctor and run frantically to God's Word instead. Hebrews 12 came alive to me during that time:

> Endure hardship as discipline; God is treating you as sons. For what son is not disciplined by his father? . . . Our

> fathers disciplined us for a little while as they thought best; but God disciplines us for our good, that we may share in His holiness. No discipline seems pleasant at the time, but painful. Later on, however, it produces a harvest of righteousness and peace for those who have been trained by it. (Hebrews 12:7, 10–11)

My faith was being tested by this ugly rash. My vanity was exposed, as I feared it would spread to my face or cause my hair to fall out. Every difficult relationship, every deficiency in my character, and every priority was put into perspective during that time. I spent a lot of time repenting. In a weird way, I felt privileged to have the Lord working so personally on me. When I drew near to Him, He drew very near to me. I had unexplainable peace—until I ventured out in public.

One of the most oppressive parts of that trial was that I was bombarded, even by Christians, with remedies for healing myself. I was exhorted to "take control of my health." I gave in a few times and spent many hours online researching diets and products people insisted would heal me. Every time I gave in to the pressure to look into these remedies, I came away feeling overwhelmed, panicked, and confused. When I drew near to Christ, on the other hand, I found peace.

There was freedom in relinquishing control of my body to my heavenly Father. Even if my kidneys were to shut down, as frightening as that would be, I knew I was in His care. That is not to say I did nothing to care for my body, but I ultimately learned through that terrifying trial to abide in faith—not to abide in self-saving. The opposite of faith is fear. Fear is a virus that is highly contagious, spreads rapidly, and easily paralyzes its victims. The anti-fear serum is faith in God. He doesn't want us to waste time worrying about our physical bodies (Matthew 6:25). It requires faith to believe His promise that He will give us exactly what we need, when we need it.

At present, this confusing illness has not given me too much grief. The Lord has given it to me as a gift to train me to abide in faith. Every now and then it shows up in some strange symptom that serves to remind me that my body is in the Lord's hands. It reminds me of my mortality and what I want to do with the time I have—mainly to pass on the true gospel to my kids and other people He has placed in my life.

So often we live our Christian life seeking earthly comfort and man's approval—which is illusive and hard to attain. Why do we desire man's approval so much more than God's? How foolish to reject God in favor of some weak human. When we set our minds on pleasing God, we become free from man's opinion—free to love with no guilt attached. Pleasing God is much simpler than pleasing man. He specifies what He is looking for in His Word. He is pleased with faith, love, and humility: "This is the one I esteem: he who is humble and contrite in spirit, and trembles at my word" (Isaiah 66:2).

Making it Stick

- Our first instinct is to react to any stressful situation by doing something about it. Yet this is the opposite of what we should do. Psalm 46:10 reminds us to "be still, and know that I am God." Next time you are tempted to *do* something as a reaction to personal pressure, practice abiding in Christ instead. Calm down. Pray. Believe.

- God doesn't bargain with behavior. As much as we would like to make deals with Him—*I'll be good, Lord, and you'll give me my reward*—He does not work like that. He won't be manipulated into fulfilling our fleshly desires. Instead, meditate on passages like Romans 8:1–6. What is true of the mind that is controlled by the Spirit (verse 6)?

8

KEEPING YOUR EYES ON CHRIST IN THE STORM

Sometimes, even grown-ups need pictures to understand concepts. Perhaps the most vivid illustration of abiding in faith from Scripture is found in Matthew chapter 14. Here we find Jesus's disciples fighting a tempest in the middle of the sea when Jesus came to them, walking on the water. Peter called out: "Lord if it's you, command me to come to you on the water." Jesus said, "Come" and Peter jumped out of the boat (see verse 28).

It must have been an exhilarating experience walking on the sea as if it were a wet sidewalk. Peter lived above his circumstances (literally) for a few minutes until something distracted him. He took his eyes off Jesus and began to look instead at the wind and the waves. He traded faith for fear and began to sink.

Peter had enough faith to get him out of the boat but not enough to keep him on top of the water, because he took his eyes off Jesus and put them on his circumstances. When he did that, Peter started to doubt that Christ was in control and that He could continue to sustain him. In that moment Peter believed his circumstances were bigger than his

God. Even while Jesus was proving that He could be trusted—Peter began to doubt.

The Wind and Waves of Female Relationships

I am part of a small committee of women who direct the women's ministries at our church. A few years back a woman began attending our church who was a very strong leader. I liked Sandra. She was a say-it-like-it-is kind of person and we became friends. Over time, however it became clear that her philosophy of ministry was very different from ours. Those of us on the committee tried to be good listeners, give her the freedom to express her views, and then talk about them without anger. Our lone request was that she discuss these differences only with the leadership so we could sort them out privately and prevent division in the body.

It wasn't long before I began to hear from other women that Sandra was slandering me and others. She was beginning to gain a following and even started her own group of ladies who met together instead of going to the Bible study at our church. On many occasions, I received phone calls from confused ladies who expressed doubts about the legitimacy of our ministry. This is a difficult situation, of course. After careful questioning, I was usually able to determine that Sandra had planted these seeds of doubt.

Betrayal from an enemy is one thing, but betrayal from someone you thought was your friend is downright painful. I confess I did not react well to this attack on my character or our ministry. I looked around at the storm brewing all around me, and I feared the waves. She even convinced some of our Bible study leaders that we should focus more time teaching domestic skills and less time in the Bible together. I was tempted on many occasions to pick up the phone and build my own army against her. I lost my temper several times when I heard about the poison she was spreading. It seemed to me that her full-time job was to bring our women's ministry down.

I spent a lot of time wrestling with the Lord about this—asking Him why He would allow such opposition to take place. I fretted over how to repair my reputation. Basically, I wasted a lot of time trying to keep myself on top of the water instead of putting my eyes on Christ and letting Him handle Sandra.

Looking back, I now see that Sandra's presence in our church drew me and other leaders close to the Lord. I finally sought His wisdom when I had no more of my own. I could not control her with anger or kindness or anything else. I could not control who would follow her and who would recognize how dangerous she was. The only thing I could do was put my eyes on Jesus and resist falling into the same trap Sandra had. My tongue could be just as deadly as hers. I could kill the gospel by focusing on stopping her. In my heart, I handed her over to the Lord to take care of, confessed my prideful anger, and became free. I learned through this "friendship" to *do* less and *believe* more.

> "DO LESS AND *BELIEVE* MORE."

In the same way that resistance and pain strengthen our muscles, trials and opposition strengthen our faith. For example, I hate to exercise. I would rather curl up with a book and a cup of coffee any day. I force myself to exercise, however, because my body needs resistance training so it will be strong and able to handle the demands of my busy life. Still, every time I'm on the elliptical, I count the minutes until I can get off—keeping in mind the benefits I will enjoy from it if I will persevere.

So it was with my relationship with Sandra—and with Christ. Anything that is to become stronger must come against resistance to do so. The Lord is the perfect trainer. He applies just the right amount of resistance to our lives that will drive us to Him. He knows how much we can handle and when it is time to rest (1 Peter 5:10). He also promises never to leave or forsake us and offers His wisdom along the way so we can endure the pain with the right perspective.

The opposition I faced from someone else's slander brought *my* sin to the surface so I could see it and repent of it. It humbled me and caused me to draw near to Christ. It caused a longing in my heart for Christ and a willingness to even be the janitor in the kingdom if that's what He was calling me to. This situation also caused the women's leadership team to seek better communication and protection from the elders of our church, which resulted in greater unity.

Ultimately, Sandra left our congregation. When it became clear that she had moved on, one of the committee members said to me: "Are you glad she's gone?" I said: "No, because there will be ten more just like her." In Acts 20:30, Paul warned the Ephesians that "even from your own number men will arise and distort the truth in order to draw away disciples after them." I should've expected it and kept my eyes on Christ from the start.

The Storm That Stretches Faith

Just as I wondered why the Lord would allow such opposition in His church, we may ask why Jesus would send His disciples out alone into a storm that He knew was approaching. Why would He allow them to struggle all night, fearing for their lives and not come to their rescue until morning? When Jesus finally did come to them He knew exactly where to find them on that vast sea. He knew their plight all along. Could it be that there was a good reason for them to suffer this hardship?

This incident took place immediately after Jesus had fed five thousand men (plus their wives and children) with just a few loaves and fish. The gospel of Mark gives insight into what was going on inside the disciples' hearts when they got into the boat that evening: "They had not understood about the loaves; their hearts were hardened" (Mark 6:52).

Jesus had a purpose in waiting to rescue his disciples. It was to soften their hearts so He could manifest His glory to them. A hard heart can never see God's glory. Very often God allows struggles in our lives to soften our hearts and to rid us of selfishness so He can reveal Himself to us and increase our faith.

> "A HARD HEART CAN NEVER SEE GOD'S GLORY."

Time to Cry Out

Peter began to sink as he focused on the overwhelming circumstances surrounding him. I pondered that phrase, *beginning to sink*, from Matthew 14:30. If I jumped out of a boat I wouldn't *begin* to sink, I would immediately sink. As Peter's faith shrank, so did his stability. But God was gracious in that He gave Peter enough time to cry out for help before he was consumed.

I suspect most Christian couples face sexual troubles sometime in the duration of their marriage. As much as the enemy tempts people to engage in sexual behavior before they are married, he tempts them to avoid it after—at least with each other. This can be the stormiest area of marriage—and the most un–talked about. The majority of counseling I have done over the years has been with women whose husbands have been unfaithful—either with a real person or with pornography. There has been a great push in the church lately to help men overcome their addictions to pornography and deviant sexual activity, but women are often left behind to work through the consequences on their own.

I don't know that a man will ever understand what pornography does to the psyche of his wife. The rejection alone sends her spiraling into a sea of head-trash. She knows she can't compete with airbrushed beauty. She obsesses over her body, thinking if she were thin enough or pretty enough this would have never happened. She blames immodest women, as if the root of his problems were somehow external. Men wonder why their wives can't just forgive and get back to the sexual relationship they used to have. She's broken in this area. Her husband doesn't understand he's the one who broke her.

Satan uses male infidelity as an opportunity to fill the female mind with untrue accusations. The emotional and mental energy it takes for her to just get through the sexual act after infidelity of any kind is excruciating. She feels like a prostitute. Her sexual desire shuts down until trust can be rebuilt—but she is told to "do it" anyway. She feels shamed into thinking his lust problem is somehow her responsibility to fix. She can't fix it because lust is never satisfied—it will never be enough.

She bears the burden of having to meet his needs, but cannot view it as anything other than a dirty selfish act. It is hard for her to share her intimate self with him knowing that she could easily be replaced by a magazine centerfold or a random woman at work. To her, the most vulnerable and spiritual act is to him merely entertainment with any warm body. Many women enter marriage already carrying this kind of baggage.

I cannot counsel these women to "just do it." Here is one of those situations where the only thing she can do is cry out to Jesus: "Lord, please rescue me!" The only "steps to healing" I can give are simple but not easy: 1) Cry out to Jesus. 2) Repent of your own sin. 3) Ask for supernatural love and forgiveness for your husband and a pure sexual desire. 4) Ask for the lies that you believe to be exposed so you can stop believing them. 5) Believe that the Lord will give you what you need, when you need it. Ask Peter—there is joy in jumping out of the boat.

I can tell her that she is never more like Christ than when she is setting aside her own desire to protect herself in order to be vulnerable with a person who does not deserve it. Never is she more like Christ than when she bears her husband's shame, feels like a prostitute, and goes through with it anyway. Not just the act itself but the love that motivates the act—that is Christlikeness. It's supernatural! So I tell her it may be a process she goes through with the Lord every time her husband approaches her. But when she cries out for a rescue—the Lord gives it and He gives it abundantly.

> "ASK PETER—THERE IS JOY IN JUMPING OUT OF THE BOAT."

I have seen the Lord give not only supernatural forgiveness but supernatural sexual desire to women who have been cheated on by their husbands. The following is the journal entry of one such woman shortly after learning of her husband's struggle with pornography. She wanted me to share it with you.

> He invited a crowd into our bedroom. I didn't know it but for years I shared his attention with others more beautiful than I. The news overwhelmed me: the realization of betrayal, memories of conversations about *other* people who struggled with this sort of thing, past denials. Part of me grieved over his secret bondage that he could not even tell me—his

closest confidant in every other area of life. The other part of me wanted to cover myself and hide from him. What did they look like? What could they offer that I could not? How could I take it any other way than that he was not attracted to me anymore? He insisted that isn't it. Why then? He said he didn't want to bother me every time he wanted me. Is it my fault, then, that I haven't been available? Have I been blind to his needs? Am I responsible for this?

I remember thinking this must be true of other women. Judgmentally in my mind thinking they must have contributed to their husband's problem by withholding sex. He's never mentioned being unsatisfied to me. It must be my body. All of a sudden I am insecure about my body. I don't want him to see me. I feel ashamed and dirty as if I've been with them too. I feel like starting at my toes and zipping all the way up under my chin. My feelings are hurt.

I don't understand men. Is that all they want? Did he think of them when he was with me? How can that *not* cross my mind every time he looks at me that way? He didn't want to bother me? With what? The things that draw me close to him and cause me to desire him? He just wanted a quick fix rather than taking the time to pursue me? What about our life together, our close late-night talks, our laughter? Was all that contrived so he could get me in the sack? I remember him escaping me many times—now I know to be with them. I'm jealous of the time he spent with them. Oh, I have to take these thoughts captive. I cry a lot. Lord, can you heal me enough to go back to my marriage bed with him? Can you restore him to lead me as a godly man? How can I be vulnerable again?

I will go to your Word for comfort. I'm free at the foot of your cross. You never reject me. Comfort me with your presence, Lord. I can't tell anyone but you. What does your Word tell me?

I scramble through passages. What comes to mind? Verses on forgiveness, yes, verses on marriage, yes, verses on love, yes. Help me, Lord, to apply these passages to me and not to him. Verses on freedom, yes, verses on suffering, yes, verses on waiting on the Lord—oh yes.

I will face this pain and insecurity with your help, Lord. I will see what good thing you will bring from it. I will pray for a supernatural forgiveness and love for my husband—for healing for two sinners committed to each other for better or worse. I will remember what you saved me from. I will lower my expectations of other people and place all my expectation upon you, Lord, for you can be trusted. Thank you for not forbidding me to come to you with the full force of my emotions. You have not turned me away in my anger. You have not rolled your eyes impatiently at my tears. You have comforted me in my despair. Let me crawl up on the mountaintop with you—don't send me down to the valley for awhile. "For you will not reject your people; you will never forsake your inheritance . . . When I said, 'My foot is slipping,' your love, O LORD, supported me. When anxiety was great within me, your consolation brought joy to my soul." (Psalm 94:14,18–19)

The Lord used this painful circumstance to bring this woman's husband to repentance. She got a better man for going through this. This is not a guarantee. Some women lose their husbands but gain a closer walk with Christ. Whatever happens, He brings forth good for those who trust in Him. I have seen marriages healed from infidelity beyond what they could ever imagine. Old grouchy married couples become like newlyweds. Young foolish couples on the brink of divorce become the most stable families in the church. It is the Lord, and the Lord only, who can do this. It is a walk of faith.

> "THE LORD WAITS FOR US TO CRY OUT TO HIM BEFORE RESCUING US TO BUILD OUR FAITH."

Just like in Peter's circumstances, the Lord waits for us to cry out to Him before rescuing us to build our faith. "Then you will call, and the LORD will answer; you will cry for help, and he will say: Here am I. . . . How gracious he will be when you cry for help! As soon as he hears, he will answer you" (Isaiah 58:9, 30:19b). He proves to each of us that He is faithful. We will begin to sink if we try to fix it ourselves.

Why Did You Doubt?

I know when I'm sitting in a chair opposite a stranger who has asked to meet with me that she is beginning to sink. I know that she has tried everything to fix her circumstances and has put off calling me for weeks. Reaching out for help is an act of desperation. The remedy for every person, no matter what she is going through, is to *believe* in her

> "THE PROBLEM WITH ANY KIND OF COUNSELING (CHRISTIAN OR SECULAR) IS THAT NO HUMAN CAN CHANGE ANOTHER PERSON'S HEART."

Savior more. My job is to sort out what lies she believes and apply the truth there. But I can't make her believe—I wish I could. The problem with any kind of counseling (Christian or secular) is that no human can change another person's heart. Secular counselors teach coping mechanisms and behavior modification. Christian counselors may teach those things in addition to God's word, but only God can change a heart.

I try to treat everyone individually but many things are the same in every case—the shroud of secrecy, the neglect in childhood, the self-protection, the wariness to trust me, the blame of someone else, a lack of time with God, an abundance of time with worldly things.

> "WE WANT GOD TO HELP US *OUT* OF OUR TRIALS BUT HE PROMISES TO HELP US *THROUGH* THEM."

Two issues that crop up all the time are doubts about God's concern and love and His ability to help us out of our trials. Satan would love to convince us that our difficult trials are proof that God does not love us or care about our lives. We think because God is not rescuing us the way we think He should, He isn't doing anything at all—or that He can't. Just the opposite is true. He uses trials to pry our hands off what we are trusting in and put them on Him. We want God to help us *out* of our trials but He promises to help us *through* them.

Jesus calmed the storm within the disciples' hearts *before* he calmed the storm all around them. He does this with us too. I am convinced we learn most things the hard way. He has to deal with our faith before He deals with our circumstances. When Jesus asked Peter, "Why did you doubt?" the answer seems obvious: *Well, I doubted because it isn't normal for a human being to stand on top of water, especially in a tempest.* It also isn't normal for a wife to forgive her unfaithful husband and find joy in the Lord through infidelity. Yet

"God is our refuge and strength, an ever-present help in trouble" (Psalm 46:1). The psalmist also says: "It was good for me to be afflicted so that I might learn your decrees" (Psalm 119:71). There is the truth—believing it is the hard part.

As Peter and Jesus walked back to the boat together and got in, the lesson was over. Jesus quickly calmed the storm and the disciples came to the conclusion they should have come to after handing out many basketfuls of loaves and fish: "Then those who were in the boat worshiped him, saying, 'Truly you are the Son of God'" (Matthew 14:33). This is the conclusion we should come to also. We will make it easier on ourselves if we don't resist what the Lord is doing.

Making it Stick

- Have you ever been tempted to believe your circumstances are too difficult for even God to figure out? Do you view difficult circumstances as punishment for sin rather than believing your punishment was taken by Jesus on the cross? What causes you to take your eyes off of Christ and put them onto your circumstances? How can you put them back on Christ?

- Jesus's disciples witnessed the miracle of feeding five thousand men plus wives and children but were unmoved because their hearts were hard (Mark 6:52). A hard heart can never see God's glory. It must be supernaturally softened by God (usually with difficult circumstances). With this in mind, why do you think Jesus refused to perform miracles in these passages? —Matthew 12:38–42, Mark 8:11–12, John 6:28–36.

9

FRIENDSHIP AND THE FEAR OF MAN (OR WOMAN)

Truth is often stranger than fiction. Flashback to high school, senior year: my friend Jennifer and I were at a party. There was a bonfire and a ton of people everywhere. Plastic cup in hand, we headed to the deck to stand in line at the keg. While we were standing there we heard a familiar voice behind us say, "Should you girls be here?" I froze with fear. We turned around to find a middle-aged woman from my church standing there. Her eyes were fixed on me. Her hand was attached to a sixteen-year-old pimple-faced boy from Jennifer's class. I could hardly process the scene. It felt like worlds colliding. I was worried that she would tell my mother—but wait, shouldn't she be worried that I would tell my mother?

This woman was the mom of one of my peers at church. We'd had youth group in her basement on several occasions. She looked like the typical church lady—short curly hair, floral dress, and large round glasses—like my mom. Turns out, she'd left her husband for this boy who was the same age as her oldest daughter—give or take a year. When my brain caught up with my eyes and I could comprehend what I was witnessing, fear left me. With this brazen act, she had declared war on people's opinion of her. Her sin was out there for everyone to see. She no longer cared if people judged her. I knew she would have no contact with anyone who would dare to snitch on me, when they had the dirt on her.

We looked each other up and down—each of us judging the other. Neither she nor I had an ounce of fear of each other or of the Lord, for that matter. The book of Proverbs says the fear of the Lord is the beginning of knowledge and wisdom but fools despise wisdom and discipline (see Proverbs 1:7, 9:10). I think it's safe to say, during that time of my life, I fit into the latter category.

I had become accustomed to a wrong understanding of God's grace—the powerless kind that waits around for fools to clean up their act. I planned to get around to it someday. In the meantime, God's judgment seemed unlikely since I continued to get away with sin. At least I wasn't as bad as her. So I thought.

Looking back, I feel compassion for her. We were in the same boat. At the time, I loved my sin and I thought all Christians were judgmental. I wonder if she had any true friends in the church—friends who were laboring in prayer for her. I wonder if anyone tried to shepherd her to repentance or if she is marked with a scarlet letter to this day. It is the kindness of God that leads us to repentance (see Romans 2:4), not judgmental snubs from Christians. Scandals like hers and mine will continue to happen in churches. Perhaps some of them could be avoided if we were free to admit our struggle with sin to each other, rather than stuff it and pretend we don't have any.

Oh, No! I'm Exposed!

Female relationships can be tricky, even in the church. They can be one of the most encouraging and enjoyable treasures this side of heaven—if only we could stop trying to control them.

Friendship and the Fear of Man (or Woman)

We desire transparency. But that desire is stifled by worry about other people's opinions. We fear we might offend someone, become offended, or say something that will be misconstrued. The tendency to gossip looms, waiting for the right moment to engage. Questions race through our minds. Do I appear godly? Have I said too much? Too little? What must so and so think of me?

> "FEMALE RELATIONSHIPS CAN BE TRICKY."

Our problems in friendship stem from this type of self-absorption and fear of man. Some try to manufacture an image that will not be rejected. But managing reputations and navigating the fickle opinions of others is an exhausting and self-centered job. At the end of the day, fake people can only have fake friendships. To have real friends, you must be willing to be real and let people in. This is risky. Once you let them in, they can hurt you.

Most women long for close friendships but shy away from their complexity. How many of us, having had a great time at girls' night out, torment ourselves afterward with things we should not have said—resolving next time to do better, talk less, and be more godly? What is the solution for the day-after-girls'-night-out regret?

Whether we talk too much or quietly hide ourselves in the crowd, the root of our turmoil is the same. We desire to be perceived a certain way. Rarely are we dismayed when our sin remains hidden. It is when everyone sees it that we fret, withdraw, and justify ourselves. Many women resolve never to be vulnerable again so they will not hurt or feel regret. But the Bible gives a joyful alternative to isolation: "If we walk in the light, as he is in the light, we have fellowship with one another, and the blood of Jesus, his Son, purifies us from all sin" (1 John 1:7).

My closest friends are those women who enjoy deep conversations about the Lord *and* are open about their sin and struggles. With them, I am free to do the same. These are the same friends I feel most comfortable being lighthearted and laughing with. We know each other well. We love each other much and extend grace, knowing each other's weaknesses. Even these friendships come upon rocky times. But biblical friendship is so rare that we cherish it when we have it. Conflict is addressed only after self-examination and the certainty that no pettiness or imagination is involved. We assume the best. Ultimately, confrontation is rare. But when it occurs, it is done privately with gentle humility and deep love.

Friendship Must Be Free

Expectations can kill friendships. I have met many newcomers who became frustrated when friendships did not develop quickly enough. While we are a welcoming church, relationships do not form overnight. They require time and effort from both parties. In addition, not all friendships can be intimate. Intimate friendships take time to maintain. No one can manage very many and still do what God is calling her to. Sometimes this is where we get into trouble.

Friendship becomes idolatry when we move from enjoying it (at every stage) to controlling it. Friendship never blossoms when one person depends on another for happiness and validation. The only person we should become dependent upon is Christ.

The flesh is never satisfied with human attention—it will never be enough. Trying to possess a person will burden her with an occupation she cannot fulfill. Further, the desired result—closeness and friendship—proves elusive as we guilt others into serving us. When jealousy and possessiveness enter the scene, trouble is sure to follow. Love does not suck everything to itself. It is free or it is not love.

Friendship and the Fear of Man (or Woman)

My first day of fifth grade, I recall being seated at a table next to a boy who was known for being mean. It didn't take long for him to start teasing me about my red hair. "Hey carrot-top!" he said. I could feel my face and ears turn red. "Why don't you shut up, stupid!" came a voice from across the table. I smiled at my defender and from that day forward she and I became best friends.

Gina defended me a lot. She was bigger than most of the kids in our class and I felt safe with her. She wasn't afraid of anyone—not even boys who tried to beat us up on the walk home from school. We did everything together for the next five years. We shared a locker all through junior high. We stayed at each other's houses on the weekends, sang into our curling irons, talked about boys, put on makeup and other typical girlie things.

Gina was content to have just one friend—me. In exchange for my friendship, she protected me from mean kids and went along with whatever I wanted to do. I, on the other hand, became increasingly restless. I wanted to make other friends and meet new people. She resisted that and hindered other girls from getting to know me. I felt trapped.

I was not mature enough to handle it well. I tried acting aloof to get her to seek other friends. I tried to be honest with her and tell her that she was smothering me. That hurt her feelings. I finally did what any other fifteen-year-old would do—ran away from the problem. I convinced my parents to let me switch high schools for my junior and senior years. I called her a week before school started to let her know she would have to find a new locker-mate. Our friendship dwindled after that.

I am not proud of how I handled that friendship. But love cannot survive in a vacuum. If we require certain actions from friends, we will be devastated when they fail to meet our expectations. If we are ruled by another's opinion, we will resent them when they don't affirm us. If our friendship is about being served, then we are pursuing an idol—not a friendship.

Sometimes adult relationships don't move beyond junior high maturity—even in the church. If we are to have biblical friendships, then we will allow God to build them. We need to recognize when to let go or give space. If we pursue a friendship that is not reciprocated, we need to set that friend free from our expectations. Believe the best about that person. Maybe she doesn't have time for one more intimate friend. Perhaps she is enduring a private trial that makes it difficult for her to engage in the pleasantries of new friendship. For whatever reason, she hasn't made time for you. Understand that God is leading you to other friends. Give grace and let her go.

> "IF WE PURSUE A FRIENDSHIP THAT IS NOT RECIPROCATED, WE NEED TO SET THAT FRIEND FREE FROM OUR EXPECTATIONS."

Friendships can so easily turn into idolatry. You cannot truly love someone if you are enslaved to her opinion of you. Idolatrous relationships always end in resentment because no one can fill the spot designed for God. Any kind of relationship becomes an idol when we pursue it for what we *believe* it can give us (constant companionship, love, security, money, status, praise, affirmation)—but can't. Idolatry is worshiping creation rather than the creator. Our hearts often deceive us about the sinfulness of this practice. We convince ourselves that we are serving others unselfishly. But people pleasing, at its root, is not concerned with what God wants. It is all about pleasing people so they will like us, or accept us, or give us praise. That is selfishness in disguise.

Friendship and the Fear of Man (or Woman)

When we worry about other people's opinions of us, we tend to work on the appearance of who we are instead of the reality. We try to look a certain way and act a certain way that will please our human idols. We stop "abiding" and we start "doing." This sort of idolatry leads to bondage—the bondage that makes you dependent on other people.

Fear God, Not Man

There was no fear in the Garden of Eden before sin. Fear and shame go hand in hand. Once Adam and Eve ate the forbidden fruit, they were racked with fear and hid from God. It's hard to say what went through Adam's mind there in the garden, but one thing is certain. He chose to please his wife rather than please God. He loved her more in that moment than he loved God. He willingly sinned and then tried to cover it up.

What do you do with your sin? Do you confess it to God and let Him take it away, or do you hide it from people? Far too often we fear our sin will be discovered by people, rather than by God.

> "FAR TOO OFTEN WE FEAR OUR SIN WILL BE DISCOVERED BY PEOPLE, RATHER THAN BY GOD."

When we feel the pull of guilt over sin committed in public, we have a choice. We can pick up the phone and do damage control with our friends, or confess it privately to the Lord. Confession allows us to leave our guilt (and our reputation) at the foot of the cross. Sometimes confessing our sins to each other is necessary but should never take the place of confessing our sins to God.

Rather than trying to fix our problems using human wisdom and striving, why don't we turn to the Lord? Instead we trust in our ability to manipulate people and circumstances and end up in an endless cycle of self-justification, failure and despair. What we don't realize is that the Lord delights in rescuing us. He would clean up the mess we have made if we would only humble ourselves, ask Him for help, and wait in faith.

The fear of man, taken to the extreme, can make people do irrational things. I have a small television in my kitchen so I can get caught up on news while I cook dinner. I catch only a fraction of news each night but one evening this headline caught my attention: "A local Christian girl murders her newborn twin sons." My heart sank. I laid down my cooking utensils and gave my full attention to the story. Somehow this young woman hid her pregnancy (with twins!) from everyone. She confessed to detectives that she did not want her parents, who were in the house with her when she gave birth, to hear the babies. So after the first one was born, she put her hand over the child's mouth and held it there until the baby fell silent and died. She did the same with the second. Then she hid their tiny bodies in a laundry basket under some blankets. Her dad later found the bodies and called the police.

Obviously, something is not right with this twenty-five-year-old woman who was raised in a local Christian church. If I were to guess what was going on in her mind, I would bet that she did not want anyone to know she was sexually active so she hid that sin with another sin—murder. She may have been in denial for the duration of her pregnancy. What she tried to hide from her parents, the whole city now knows.

This young woman displayed her fear of man by hiding the evidence of her sin (albeit not very well) from her parents. She proved to have a greater fear of them than she had of God, who was present in the room when she snuffed out the life of her tiny sons.

So what does it mean to *fear* the Lord? Are we to literally be afraid of God? The answer is yes and no. Those who do not have a saving relationship with Jesus Christ should literally be afraid of God's eventual punishment.

For Christians, the punishment for sin was borne by Christ on the cross. They don't have to be afraid of God's eternal judgment, but may have to face consequences here on earth. God has provided a way for our sins to be removed and therefore also our fear of death and punishment. But there is a difference between punishment and discipline. When a believer falls into a pattern of sin, God will discipline her out of that sin. Discipline is meant for training—not punishment. It is painful, but it is for our good. God disciplines those He loves (Hebrews 12:6).

A proper understanding of this removes the fear of man for the believer. "In God, whose word I praise, in God I trust; I will not be afraid. What can mortal man do to me?" (Psalm 56:4). The answer to the psalmist's question is: *nothing*! The one who draws near to Christ is free from the opinions of people, the burden of sin, from fear of death and punishment—she is truly free! "There is no fear in love. But perfect love drives out fear, because fear has to do with punishment" (1 John 4:18).

True Accountability

Even though we are called to live in freedom (Galatians 5:1), our enemy loves to sow seeds of discord in our midst in order to hinder the gospel and put us in bondage to the fear of man. If he can distract us with mistreatment, we will become ineffective and divisive. One Sunday morning someone pulled me aside in the hallway at church and said, "Marci, last week you passed by me without saying hello or even looking me in the eye. I feel like you are judging me by not forgiving me." (Months before, this person had asked my forgiveness for some hypocrisy that I had witnessed. I readily gave it and then forgot about it.)

I was flabbergasted. I did not see the need to forgive this person in the first place because she had not sinned against me, but I had given it. My thoughts raced back to the previous week. I remembered being preoccupied by some other issue. I hadn't recalled passing her by; I was so immersed in my own thoughts. While I may have needed to be confronted on my self-absorption, I did not hold any grudge against this person. I asked, "Did you say hello to me?" The answer was no. Assumptions were made based on my facial expression and lack of eye contact. I was glad to have the opportunity to correct the mistake. We talked it through and the misunderstanding was cleared.

> "READING FACES IS A BAD IDEA. WHY? BECAUSE OUR CONCLUSIONS ARE USUALLY WRONG."

I cannot blame this person. I have done the same thing to others. Reading faces is a bad idea. Why? Because our conclusions are usually wrong. The apostle Paul exhorts us to only think about things that are true (Philippians 4:8). Rather than assuming or imagining motivations and attitudes, why not communicate? Why assume someone's troubled look has anything to do with you? Why not ask her if she is okay? If you are concerned about tension in a relationship—*ask*. Paul says in Romans 12:18, "If it is possible, as far as it depends on you, live at peace with everyone." If you ask, and she says there is no conflict, then you must believe her and move on.

I have an extraordinary imagination. I can teach a class and read every face in the room. If I tried to figure out what this or that look meant, I would drive myself crazy. I have learned to leave the results of my teaching, as well as individual conversations, at the foot of the cross. There are no do-overs. Therefore I have to trust the Lord. I have

Friendship and the Fear of Man (or Woman)

to believe Him when He says all things work together for good (see Romans 8:28). All things means *all* things.

The gospel sets us free from the fear of man. It liberates us from unnecessary rules and expectations we impose on each other. There is no time for pettiness between Christians (Ephesians 4:1–3). Selfishness forces the gospel into dormancy while we squabble amongst ourselves, defending our preferences and looking out for our own reputation. Friendship must originate at the foot of the cross, begin with humility and be fueled by the love that the Lord demonstrated toward us. John 15:12–13 tells us, "My command is this: Love each other as I have loved you. Greater love has no one than this, that he lay down his life for his friends." Selflessness is biblical friendship.

Putting Friendship in Its Place

Early one Saturday I got a call from my friend's husband. He wanted to make sure I would be home that evening because, he said, "my wife is going to need to talk to you." I assured him that I would be, thought nothing more of it, and went to Walmart to do some shopping. But while walking through the cards-and-party section, I suddenly felt feverish and ill. I left my cart, hurried home, and collapsed beside the porcelain throne. It was violent. I was dizzy from nausea. I spent the night passing out in intervals and waking up to my reflection and the smell of toilet water.

Meanwhile, sure enough, my friend called. She was sobbing through the phone to my husband. He looked helplessly at me and apologized to her. He knew I wouldn't be able to talk. Through a fog, I realized something terrible had happened, and I could not be there for my friend. The next morning I was fine physically, but my heart was aching. I called her. In the next moments, I heard the devastation of the previous evening. She had come home from choir practice to find her husband on his knees, weeping, with the Bible open in front of him. Through tears and repentance, he confessed to a long-term affair with another woman. Then he left to go stay with friends. He knew she would need someone to talk to and had assumed that person would be me.

Since I wasn't available, she spent the night in prayer and worship—playing her piano and crying out to God for comfort. She received it from Him first and later from me. Wild horses could not have kept me away from her any other time; if it hadn't have been for that virus, I would have been at her house within minutes. But I could never have ministered to her the way the Lord did that night. He had to force me out of the way so she would turn to Him.

Proverbs 18:24 says, "A man of many companions may come to ruin, but there is a friend who sticks closer than a brother." This friend was closer than a sister to me. I would have done anything for her. However, the Lord did not want us to put each other before Him. We were to enjoy our friendship, not worship it. We were to come to Him with our neediness first, and then to each other. She and I both learned a valuable lesson through that experience—she more than me. "Those who seek the LORD lack no good thing. . . . The righteous cry out, and the LORD hears them; he delivers them from all their troubles. The LORD is close to the brokenhearted and saves those who are crushed in spirit" (Psalm 34:10b, 17–18).

It is tempting to turn to people first rather than to God when trying circumstances hit. But seeking godly people is not the same thing as seeking God. Godly people can give advice from the Bible but they cannot soften hearts or change circumstances. I have learned to cry out to God first, then go to godly people (if I still need to). God gives both counsel and the power to heed that counsel. Friends are a gift from the Lord, but they can never take the place of our relationship with God.

Making it Stick

- Spouting off—with opinions, gossip, unsolicited advice, and more—can cause a lot of trouble, much of it hidden in hurt feelings and bitter resentment. Be mindful of the psalmist who wrote, "May the words of my mouth and the meditation of my heart be pleasing in your sight, O LORD" (Psalm 19:14). Sometimes we use this excuse: "I am the kind of person who speaks my mind. That is just who I am!" What does Galatians 5:13–15 say on the one hand about freedom and on the other about the consequences of reckless tongues among believers?

- Think about your friendships. Do you have any friends toward whom you harbor bitterness because they are not meeting your expectations? Do you think more about how you can serve them or how you want them to serve you? Are you more concerned with people's opinion of you—or God's? When you find yourself frustrated that you cannot control someone else, you may run to the cross and find freedom in relinquishing that desire to Christ, who is in control of all.

10

THE TRUTH ABOUT WOMEN AND MEN

Relationships are important to women. Of all the things we make idols out of, most women idolize human relationships more than anything else. Even more than friendships, women worship "love." We are continually fed the lie from our culture that a romantic relationship is the key to our happily ever after. This is evidenced in the amount of effort that goes into wedding plans. Girls start planning their wedding in their early teens. This kind of worship is commonplace even in the church.

> "WOMEN IDOLIZE HUMAN RELATIONSHIPS MORE THAN ANYTHING ELSE."

Idolatry and Worship

The unexpected twist in this kind of worship is that once we find relationships that are safe and satisfying (the very thing we think we need to make us happy) *we fear losing them*. When we fear losing them, we try to control them even more. Fear causes us to grab hold of what we worship. That is a good thing if what we worship is God.

But too often we grab hold of human relationships instead. Ironically, human relationships can die that way—from suffocation.

As a young woman I believed that once I had a ring on my finger, all my fears of being alone would disappear. When I fell in love with my husband, he was everything I ever wanted in a man. My happily ever after had arrived. Surprisingly, I found that instead of disappearing, my fear grew more powerful. It had taken me so long to find this man that now I feared losing him. If he came home late from the office without calling me, I would become an emotional wreck thinking he was dead in a ditch somewhere.

This was not good for our marriage. I couldn't keep tabs on him wherever he went and it made him feel like I was his mother rather than his wife. Once I had children, my fear multiplied even more. It's a full-time job just keeping preschoolers alive. I became an overprotective, controlling mom. All of this was my effort to avoid suffering the loss of someone I love. But the Lord has revealed to me since then that I don't have as much control over the lives of my loved ones as I think I do.

I spent a lot of time alone in the early years of our marriage as my husband got his career off the ground. In my loneliness, I learned, quite by accident, to draw near to the Lord. This was the benefit of being involved in a ladies' Bible study at church. We always had lessons to complete and I wanted to be prepared. I looked forward to the fellowship and, quite honestly, the free childcare. I found comfort from God's Word and the other women. As His truth grew within me, my fears had less and less of a hold on me. I began to consciously believe that He would give me the grace to go through whatever was in my future. I could leave my worry for my loved ones at the foot of the cross.

The fear of the Lord is the beginning of wisdom in every area of life. Wisdom grows as the Word implants in our hearts through faith and ignites worship. Through His Word we gain a better understanding of God *and* of ourselves. The true worshiper understands glimpses of God's grace and how undeserved it is. She has a proper fear of God's wrath, coupled with the joy that she has escaped it and has inherited His mercy instead. She understands the purpose of God's pruning hand: that He is constantly plucking idols off the throne of her heart where He belongs.

Manipulation Versus Self-Sacrifice

What do you need to do in order to get what you think you need from your man? The "Mars and Venus" guy introduced us to our internal differences as men and women. He proposed that if we really understood what the opposite sex needed, then each party would happily fulfill that need. One heading in his book reads: "How to get the support you need from your spouse with minimal sacrifice."

If his theory is true then every single one of us should be wearing a size six. If all we need to do is *understand*, then follow-through is no problem, right? We understand what it takes to be thin, so why aren't we? In the various moments throughout our day we don't *want* to do what it takes. We don't *want* to deny ourselves.

Don't get me wrong, it is helpful to understand how the opposite sex thinks. Understanding can fuel forgiveness and compassion, but the main problem in marriages is not that we don't understand what the other person needs. It's that we don't want to give it. Our sin is the problem. Bring two sinners together and the mountain of sin between them is over-shadowed only by the blindness they have toward their own sin and the clarity toward their partner's.

Lies and Expectations

I recently rented a popular chick flick to see what all the excitement was about among tweenage girls. It's about a vampire who (by the way, has no soul) falls in love with a mortal. This handsome and mysterious vampire is tormented in the presence of his mortal muse. He longs to drink her blood. It will kill her if he indulges. But his desire to ravage her is controlled by his "love." He is willing to sacrifice his own desires and remain in agony just to be in her presence.

I don't even know where to begin. This movie is like porn for women. Every one of us has fantasized about receiving this kind of admiration. The takeaway is this: there are (incredibly gorgeous) men out there who are willing to sacrifice themselves and live in torment just for the honor of being in a woman's presence. Not just any woman, she must be troubled and moody. The more emotional she is, the more he desires her. Nothing is required of her except to allow him the privilege of admiring her beauty and listening to her fears. True love drives him to protect her from his own kind. He forfeits his own happiness to serve her night and day.

This movie portrays a sexually charged, perverted version of unconditional love—what every woman is looking for but will not find in a man. This is the classic Satanic lie to women in its rawest form. It makes us believe that we are empowered by our sexuality, that we can purchase this kind of love with it. But it is slavery in disguise. Once we attach this fantasy to a man, he is on a set course toward failure. He could never live up to the vision we have created in our imagination. The female life ambition then, is to prove (to ourselves and others) that we are worthy of this kind of attention. We will do anything to find it. We exercise. We diet. We clothe ourselves with the latest bobbles. We work hard to become "good women" worthy of love. We shackle ourselves to the world's ideal. However "good" we look—that is how "good" we are.

> "ONCE WE ATTACH THIS FANTASY TO A MAN, HE IS ON A SET COURSE TOWARD FAILURE."

When you add to this the lies that men believe (and *their* version of pornography), it is no wonder disillusionment in marriage is so prevalent. Both parties head into it with thoughts on how they will be served. What a rude awakening to our sinful flesh when the gospel bids us come and serve, give and die.

Relationships, Hollywood Style

No wonder so many young women ask me how I knew my husband was "the one." Hollywood tells them it's just a matter of making sure you find "the right one." If things don't work out, it's because you didn't find "the one." Keep looking. Start over with someone new. Surely he's out there somewhere. We can clearly see Hollywood's track record for long-lasting relationships. Yet we continue to believe its lies.

Even after I became a Christian, I was a terrible judge of character and never picked men who were good for me. One day, I stopped picking and asked the Lord to help me wait for the man *He* had for me. I set aside all of my manipulative ways and even though I was interested in my husband for months before he asked me out, I waited on the Lord (not very patiently) to give him to me. Even though he was and is "the right one," we have both had plenty of pain in our marriage.

Today's young women analyze relationships so much that they can't even enjoy getting to know someone without interviewing him for marriage. They want to be sure before they commit that they can avoid any kind of suffering in marriage. Boyfriends get disqualified when it turns out they

> "TODAY'S YOUNG WOMEN ANALYZE RELATIONSHIPS SO MUCH THAT THEY CAN'T EVEN ENJOY GETTING TO KNOW SOMEONE WITHOUT INTERVIEWING HIM FOR MARRIAGE."

are not Jesus. We can't control our future like that and we can't avoid suffering in marriage. Dying to yourself is painful no matter who it's with. We don't even think to ask the Lord to lead us much less *let* Him (James 4:2–3). Resting in faith and surrendering control is sometimes the hardest thing for Christian women to do.

This Isn't The Way It Was Supposed To Be

The idea of a "happy marriage" was reinvented not by Hollywood, but by the onslaught of the gospel. In the beginning, God gave Adam a wife to bring him joy. Marital bliss was defined in the garden but lost in the fall. Part of Eve's curse was that she would desire to possess her husband but he would dominate her instead. It didn't take long for marriages to fall to abuse, neglect, male cruelty, and female rebellion.

Throughout history and in most cultures since, marriages were arranged as social contracts for the purpose of peace treaties, reproduction, and sheer convenience. Women needed protection and provision. Men needed, well . . . sexual release, and someone to bear children and take care of domestic duties. Most women throughout history have had no concept of romance. Most men have not known what loving companions their wives could be.

The gospel showed up and undid what sin and selfishness had done to marriage. From the seed of joy stemming from forgiveness in Christ, sacrificial love blossomed. When the apostles preached on Biblical marriage, the men must have been shocked by the command to love their wives and be monogamous. Being friends with your wife back then was unheard of. As the gospel transformed individuals, it inevitably transformed marriages. It is the Christian faith that pushes forth the possibility of a fulfilling marriage through selfless love. But the world always steps in with its lies and redefines the path for getting there.

Jean is a recovering addict in her sixties. She's had three failed marriages and has been living in rehab institutions for the last two years. I teach a Bible study where she currently resides. She's politely quiet when I talk about the power of the gospel to her. I can feel her disagreement.

"I know I can sort things out if I just have some time to work it out in my mind," she said. She was critical of the younger addicts in the house. "They didn't wash the dishes correctly and I told them so! What is wrong with them? I can't imagine anyone messing up her life in her twenties. I was married and had a baby when I was in my twenties."

"My life was a complete ruin by the time I was twenty-one," I said. "Only the gospel can transform anyone at any age."

She was quiet. "Well, I tell you what. I'm not giving up on love." She said. "I know I can make marriage work next time."

This time I was quiet. I marveled at the ability of the human heart to believe lies about itself and yet see others' shortcomings so clearly. How determined it is to demand love and respect from others yet angrily withhold the same from them. Jean believes, given enough time, she can figure out how to manipulate a man to give her what she thinks she needs. While stubbornly holding to her belief in human love, she rejects the offer of unconditional love and forgiveness the Lord has offered her countless times. What is her great sin? Drug addiction? Divorce? No, it is unbelief.

Scripture tells us we will find our life when we lose it (Matthew 10:39). The love we long for cannot come in human form. The Lord wants to heal women like Jean but she refuses His kind of healing. "I long to redeem them but they speak lies against me. They do not cry out to me from their hearts but wail upon their beds" (Hosea 7:13–14). Most women would rather "wail upon their beds" trying to control their own destinies than cry out to God for help.

Why do we put our hope for happiness in something that has never satisfied before? Women cannot *make* men love them. So much marital conflict is stirred by a demand to be loved, respected, or served. Impatience is the insanity that continues to demand the same thing in the same way and receive the opposite. Boil it all down and it is a flat refusal to suffer.

Suffering in Marriage

I have watched women submit to the call of suffering in their marriages for the sake of the gospel (1 Peter 2:21). I've watched others refuse and walk away. The ones who persevere with the Lord discover that somehow giving up the demand to be loved sets us free to pursue loftier goals.

First Peter chapter 3 is written to women who are suffering in their marriages. Peter encourages wives to suffer "in the same way" as Christ (1 Peter 3:1). Christ did not retaliate. He made no threats. Instead, He "entrusted himself to him who judges justly" (1 Peter 2:23). This chapter rails against every natural inclination a woman possesses. We think we have to keep talking until we are understood; it says he may be won over without words. We think he will respond to criticism and shame tactics; it says you will reach him with pure and reverent behavior. We think we can woo him with outward beauty; it says beauty should come from the inner self.

> "SOMEHOW GIVING UP THE DEMAND TO BE LOVED SETS US FREE TO PURSUE LOFTIER GOALS."

When we bring our neediness to Christ, He gives the peace and love we have been seeking from our husbands. We can talk to the Lord as much as we want without losing His attention. He can absorb all of our emotions and steady us with His peace. "You will keep in perfect peace him whose mind is steadfast, because he trusts in you" (Isaiah 26:3).

Confessions of a Bible Teacher

Christians do not outgrow the gospel. They don't achieve a level of righteousness and then write how-to books to help the folks who haven't figured it out yet. We never get beyond needy. I was asked to teach a series on the power of the gospel as it plays out in the various areas of a woman's life. When the time came to teach on marriage, my own marriage was in conflict. For months, every struggle we have had in our nearly twenty-year marriage (plus a few more) came to a climax and remained unresolved. Imagine my desire to fix this quickly before I had to stand in front of a group of people and teach about the power of the gospel in marriage!

> "WE NEVER GET BEYOND NEEDY."

It wasn't for a lack of trying that the impasse remained. My husband and I sought the Lord individually and together more often during that time than we had in our entire marriage. Both of us confessed our sin (at least the sin we knew about) openly to the Lord, to each other, and even to other people. We believed, given enough time and conversation, we could fix it. Every time the subject came up though, resolve seemed cloudy and just out of reach. When the subject did not come up, our hearts became heavy bags of wet sand weighed down with small talk. We avoided eye contact for fear of what we might find if we looked too closely. We asked the Lord for enough strength for that day to fulfill our duties . . . and we waited.

As I prayed about how I could possibly teach on this subject, it became clear it would be a good time to apply the gospel to my own marriage. This was exactly the time I should write about it and teach it. It is humbling to share some of these personal matters with the world, but I hope every chapter in this book will ring loudly with the message to stop *doing* stuff and start *believing* the gospel more. Trials that are confusing and impossible to figure out with human wisdom should not take us by surprise. In fact, they lead us to the cross through the wake of failed self-help methods, shallow advice, and every tactic we use to escape suffering.

You would think that because we both wanted resolution, and because we both love the Lord and each other, fixing these issues would be easy. "Just talk it out and come to an understanding of each other," I can hear someone say. Nope! We were not able to fix it with lots of talking, tears, or silence. Both of us thought to ourselves: *Why can't you do better? Why can't you be more like me?* Twenty years into my walk with the Lord, I still need to return to the power of the gospel—I always will. As I taught on the power of the gospel in marriage that night, the Lord required me to put my marriage on the altar, humble myself, and wait for His wisdom. He required me to trust Him that the solution was cloudy for a reason.

In the meantime, He revealed hidden sin in my heart—things that make me hard to lead. He revealed sin in my husband's heart—things that make him hard to follow. It is during times like this that the wealth of Scripture rushes in to support and comfort us. Our weakness forces us to depend on His strength. Staring at each other with tear-stained faces, we clung to this truth.

Because this book is for women, I will leave what my husband learned for some other writer to address. But maybe some women can glean from my experience. I am still learning to humble myself. The Lord is not calling me to be my husband's life coach. I can give my opinion and talk things through with him, but it emasculates him when I tell him what to do—it disables him from leading. It makes him want to give up and not try. Wives who point out "areas of improvement" do not help a man to improve. In fact, the contrary is true.

Realizing that I do this, I have been praying that the Lord would mold my husband into the man *He* is calling him to be, rather than the man I think he should be. The Lord is answering that prayer by shoving me out of the way, putting His divine hand over my mouth, and making my husband face some things alone.

Most of us learn everything the hard way. The "obedience that comes from faith" (Romans 1:5) is a willing acceptance of the Scripture, even when human wisdom tells us to do the opposite. The gospel is not about doing better or requiring our spouse to do better. Letting perseverance have its work means humbling ourselves and submitting to whatever trial the Lord brings. The sooner we take our expectations of marriage to the cross, the sooner we will be free from the vortex of unfulfilled human ideals.

> "MOST OF US LEARN EVERYTHING THE HARD WAY."

A Not So Rare Extreme

My comments regarding marriage thus far have been made to the majority of Christian women who wrestle with common frustrations and struggles in marriage. But I feel the need to address extreme cases for fear that some will mistake this message on suffering in marriage for a command to cover sin and abuse. Occasionally I encounter women who are suffering in their marriages due to on-going verbal, mental, sexual, and even physical abuse. It takes me a long time to discover abuse in "Christian" homes because, on the one hand, these women want help, but on the other, they are so fearful they don't trust anyone to give it.

Counseling women in this situation is much like swimming out to save a drowning person. Once they find someone who affirms they are not crazy but are experiencing real abuse, they grab hold of that person as their potential savior instead of holding on to Christ. It requires care to help them—they are terrified. They are fragile. Their spouse is volatile and resentful of any intrusion into their lives.

Usually a wife in this situation truly loves her husband and worries *he* will get hurt. This is why she helps him cover his sin, therefore enabling him to continue in it. She may passive-aggressively share bits and pieces of her struggle with different people—hinting that all is not well. I believe what motivates this is a secret hope that a godly man will take notice, carefully befriend her husband, and love him into changed behavior without really knowing about (or addressing) his sin. Her expectations of this scenario grow and spill onto those around her. Some may even pursue a friendship with him but are never able to get very deep.

It is Biblical for younger women to seek counsel from older women. But when real abuse is discovered, it is essential for her to turn to the male leadership of the church for help. The hard part is getting her to trust men. It is unthinkable for her to tell men what goes on inside her home. She knows she will pay a heavy price for bringing someone from the outside in. Her husband controls her with anger and he depends upon secrecy to keep it that way. It is for this type of situation the following passage was given:

> If you brother sins against you, go and show him his fault, just between the two of you. If he listens to you, you have won your brother over. But if he will not listen, take one or two others along, so that "every matter may be established by the testimony of two or three witnesses." (Matthew 18:15–16)

Any wife in this situation will be terrified at this advice—but that is where faith comes in. She will need to walk by faith and not by sight, praying fervently through each day. There's a right and a wrong way to go about this. Giving bits and pieces of information to different people will not biblically expose the sin. It will be mistaken for slander rather than a cry for help, increasing the confusing nature of this kind of trial. As an act of faith in this prescriptive passage, she should present her situation to one or two of the elders in her church. She needs to give the full story—including her own sin and exactly what she is afraid of.

Before embarking on this very difficult act of faith, she should evaluate her motives. Slander is motivated by a vengeful desire to destroy another person; instead her desire should be a loving intention to bring her husband to repentance. No human being will be her savior—no person can do what only God can do. It requires patience to wait upon God and follow the steps He has given her. She can entrust herself to Him who judges justly, no matter what her husband's response may be.

Ultimately, each situation has its own unique set of circumstances that cannot be addressed here. But the bottom line is, we are not meant to walk the Christian life alone. No matter how much you suffer in your marriage, drawing near to Christ will make you less needy. This is not to manipulate your husband to change or to spend more time with you. Christ fulfills your need for unconditional love. As you learn to abide in Christ, you will not require your husband to fulfill all your needs (which he cannot do anyway) and you will cease to believe the lie that he can. When Christ fills your cup to overflowing, then the quality of your marriage will not define the happiness or unhappiness of your day.

> "WE ARE NOT MEANT TO WALK THE CHRISTIAN LIFE ALONE."

Misunderstandings will always be a regular part of marriage and relationships in general. But we do not need to be consumed with how to escape suffering. We learn to embrace it as beneficial for spiritual growth. The Lord can be trusted to take care of us and protect us from enduring more than we can handle (1 Corinthians 10:13).

> "AS YOU LEARN TO ABIDE IN CHRIST, YOU WILL NOT REQUIRE YOUR HUSBAND TO FULFILL ALL YOUR NEEDS (WHICH HE CANNOT DO ANYWAY) AND YOU WILL CEASE TO BELIEVE THE LIE THAT HE CAN."

The "Mars and Venus" guy gives lists and lists of stuff to *do* to improve your marriage. Instead, do one thing, superwoman. Give up your manipulation and draw near to Christ in your weakness. Receive His strength. Watch Him work. "True worshipers will worship the Father in spirit and truth, for they are the kind of worshipers the Father seeks" (John 4:23).

Making it Stick

- Have you ever believed the key to your "happily ever after" would be found in a romantic relationship? Do you fear never finding "the right one"? If you have found "the right one," do you fear losing him? Do you believe the lie that you accidentally married "the wrong one" and that there is a "right one" that you missed out on?

- First Peter chapter 3 speaks of "holy women of the past who put their hope in God." Abraham's wife Sarah is specifically mentioned. Read Genesis chapter 20. How did Sarah entrust herself to God even when her husband didn't? How did God show Himself faithful to her even when her husband failed her?

11

ABIDING IN HUMILITY

A large portion of this book is devoted to how the gospel transforms every area of a Christian's life through belief in Jesus Christ. Only through faith does a display of genuine Christ-like behavior emerge. Many pages have been devoted to how this plays out in relationships. However, relationships do not change on a horizontal level until there is clarity on the vertical (between God and people). We were created to worship God.

Adam and Eve enjoyed perfect fellowship with God and one another until Satan deceived Eve into believing God was holding out on her. It was an attractive thought to "be like God, knowing good and evil" (Genesis 3:5): if she could be like God, she would no longer need God. Human pride was born that day. The way to defeat it was with divine humility.

A Different Kind of Toy Story

As children, many of us fantasized about our toys coming to life and playing with us. There have been many movies based on this premise. The toys in the movies show complete loyalty and love to their owner. It is their job as toys, after all, to bring happiness to their owner. In the movies they embrace this job wholeheartedly.

Suppose when you were a kid, you had the power to bring your toys to life. You dreamt of how lovingly they would respond to you and now they could. You knew they would be grateful that you brought them to life and would trust you to take care of them and love them in return. Their greatest joy was to be chosen to be played with.

However, one day you left for a while and when you came back, you found them fighting with one another. Barbie and Ken moved to opposite sides of the dream house. G.I. Joe un-stuffed all the teddy bears just for fun. Even your favorite doll, Mrs. Beasley, behind those square glasses, digressed into a bitter rabble-rouser. Chaos ensued in your room. Pretty soon they became so violent that they began to kill each other. They stopped talking to you and ignored your pleas for them to stop. Not only did they not want to play with you, they didn't want to have anything to do with you.

What would you do? Would you not have the right to get a garbage bag, load them all up and throw them away and start over with new toys? After all, they are your toys. You might think twice before bringing any more toys to life. You would never consider putting on plastic flesh and becoming one of them in order to reason with them. You definitely would not let them kill *you*. This illustration has many flaws. We can't even begin to put ourselves "in God's shoes." But it does illustrate the incomprehensible humility and love it took for Jesus to even consider coming to walk among us.

The Humility of the Incarnation

Every year we celebrate the humility of Christ at Christmas—or do we? Sometimes I wonder if the Christmas story has become so familiar that its true impact has been exchanged for cheap sentimentality. We sugarcoat the cruelty and the unsanitary conditions of that night with pictures of quaint stables on calm snowy nights. Maybe that's the only way we can cope with the unsettling injustice of it all. God came to us but we left Him out in the cold and filth with the animals.

We sing about angels and shepherds swooning over a child sleeping peacefully on a cozy bed of hay. But the reality is, the angels and the lowlifes of society were the only ones who recognized Him. The Savior was rejected by His own people from day one, and the crude nature of His birth was proof of that. Even in His infancy He suffered. The reputation of being an illegitimate child followed Him throughout His life. The most astonishing thing about all this is . . . He chose to come to us this way.

It's ironic that of all times of the year we should spend time in reflection—thinking and meditating on the incarnation—most of us instead degenerate into a mad rush of self-indulgence, expectations, and busyness. Regular schedules get shelved in early November so Christmas traditions can take center stage in priority.

It is our responsibility as mothers to make sure our children have a "good Christmas." In our culture a good Christmas equals *stuff*. Usually by the end of the season the children are fighting over big plastic toys and the adults, in a more subtle fashion, struggle internally over some dissatisfaction about how their Christmas turned out. I know for myself, when January rolls around I am relieved to put away the tinsel and return to my close walk with the Lord—vowing next year I won't get so far away from Him.

Gift giving at Christmas started as a remembrance of the greatest gift of all time. It began with God, who forged a plan that no man could imagine because it is so contrary to human nature.

The plan was this: God would humble Himself in order to save prideful man.

A Humble God?

I minored in art history in college. A large portion of my study was the investigation of images various people groups crafted for the purpose of worship. It is an extraordinary phenomenon to observe from this vantage point. People all over the world and throughout history have had this need in common—to worship something. Certain things were out of their control (weather, life and death, illness, and so on); they figured someone needed to be appeased in order to give them what they wanted. Therefore, they created gods and entire religious systems in order to earn some favor with a deity they knew must exist. Not coincidentally, these deities all possessed some wickedness that must be pacified. If you were to investigate all the religions of the world throughout history, except for Christianity, you will never find a humble god. In the human mind humility and power do not go together. It is an altogether foreign concept.

Philippians 2 chronicles the descent of the Lord Jesus Christ "who, being in very nature God, did not consider equality with God something to be grasped, but . . . humbled himself and became obedient to death—even death on a cross!" (vv. 6–8). With all the sermons that could be preached from these verses about the deity of Christ, one striking message clangs loudly against our human wisdom—God humbled Himself!

> "WE CAN EITHER HUMBLE OURSELVES OR BE HUMBLED. WHICH WOULD YOU PREFER?"

Later in Philippians, Paul instructs us to *let our attitude be like that* (see Philippians 2:5). How hard it is for us to direct our thoughts and emotions toward truth so our attitude will willingly yield. How often are we willing to humble ourselves and become obedient—much less to death? We can either humble ourselves or be humbled. Which would you prefer?

Bait and Switch

I was at a baby shower one evening—a common social gathering for the women of our church. At the punch table, an acquaintance and fellow church member asked me if I would like to have lunch with her the following week. I happily agreed. The following week we sat in a girlie-type restaurant eating great food and enjoying our conversation. When the check arrived we each plopped down a credit card. As I was gathering my things to leave my lunch partner suddenly changed her tone.

"Marci, I wanted to tell you that I have stopped attending Bible study and so have three other women I have talked to." I could feel my face flush. I knew this tone well, but at this moment, it had caught me off guard. *Don't be defensive, Marci. Don't be defensive*, I said to myself.

"We all feel like you come across as angry when you teach. I feel like you preach more than teach and as a result none of us feel like coming anymore," she said. I wanted to ask her what the difference was between "preaching" and "teaching" and what I should change in order to turn one into the other, but I remained quiet.

The problem with trying not to be defensive is that there is no defense against words stabbing your unguarded heart. It was physically painful to hear any more of her words but I had to sit there as she elaborated on my failures. My eyes filled up and overflowed with tears. I tried to blink them away quickly so she wouldn't be able to tell I was hurt, but there was no hiding it. I asked her if she would please tell me who the other women were so I wouldn't look around church and wonder who these three mystery dissenters were. She wouldn't say.

I reminded her that I was only one of several rotating teachers. Did she feel the same way about them? She did not. I apologized and told her I would seek accountability in this area. She seemed unmoved and cold—maybe even a little smug.

When the waitress brought back our receipts, her tone changed again. "This was so much fun," she said. "We should do this once a month. I know of a really fun artsy restaurant we should try next month."

I didn't say it out loud but in my heart, I thought, *I will never have lunch with you again.*

When I got home I was devastated. It didn't help that I had to teach Bible study that same evening. I don't know why I took her criticism so hard—I guess because it was so unexpected. Usually I can tell when someone has an agenda like that. It was a bait and switch. I begged the Lord to help me get through this one last Bible study and then I would reevaluate if I should be teaching at all.

That evening, with fear and trembling I taught from the book of Romans. My emotions were so raw I felt like I had been stripped naked and pushed to the front of the room. When I finished the closing prayer I looked up. I understood what the faces of the women staring back at me were expressing. I was feeling the same thing. I don't know what happened that night but it was powerful—even I could see that. I knew for a fact that power didn't come from me. I wasn't exhilarated like I had been in the past when I could tell that God had showed up. I was still fragile, but in that moment I understood that it was *necessary* for me to be stripped for that power to be unleashed.

Paul shared in 2 Corinthians that his thorn in the flesh was given to him to keep him from becoming conceited. "That is why, for Christ's sake, I delight in weaknesses, in insults, in hardships, in persecutions, in difficulties. For when I am weak, then I am strong" (2 Corinthians 12:10). If Paul could delight in his very real persecutions, I could get over myself and delight in getting my feelings hurt every now and then. I thought, *Maybe I will have lunch with her once a month, or maybe once a week.*

Conflicts like this are a regular occurrence in my life. I don't like drama but I have come to see it as necessary to keep me dependent on Christ and not the gifts He has given me. I don't have the power to soften a hard heart—that power comes only from God's word and the Holy Spirit. Sometimes *my* heart is the one that needs softening. Sometimes the women I spend the most time pouring my life into end up being the most resentful toward me. I recognize that I am not to gather followers unto myself so they become dependent on me, but I am to lead people to follow Christ.

The Power of Restraint

Maybe one of the greatest works the Holy Spirit has to do in me on a regular basis is to bridle my tongue when I'm angry or hurt. In my natural state, my personality can bulldoze almost anyone. Restraining me must be like holding back a team of wild horses. One remarkable fact about Jesus is that when He walked on this earth, He never exerted His power for selfish reasons. Satan tempted Him to make stones into bread after He had fasted for forty days. That does not sound unreasonable—He could have done that easily but He did not. He submitted Himself to the Father's will in everything.

> "JESUS NEVER EXERTED HIS POWER FOR SELFISH REASONS."

Think about this. Jesus's whole life was plagued by those who mocked Him and hated Him. At any time Jesus had the power to kill an entire multitude with a word. He healed people from blindness. He could've just as easily afflicted others with blindness or any other malady. If we had this kind of power at our disposal, would we be able to restrain ourselves from using it for our own purposes? I am quite sure I would be surrounded by blind people begging me for a reversal.

> "HE SUBMITTED HIMSELF TO THE FATHER'S WILL."

Think about the restraint Jesus maintained throughout His whole life—entrusting Himself to the will of the Father and suffering unjustly at the hands of evil men. He had a greater purpose than living for His own happiness—He was here to die.

Can You See It?

There's a massive painting in The (Salvador) Dali Museum in St. Petersburg, Florida. It's an impressive thirty feet high by twenty feet wide landscape of a woman from behind (nude, of course) standing on a veranda looking out at a valley. It's one of Dali's technical masterpieces. Its details are meticulous. What's more impressive, however, is what happens to all those details when you turn around and walk about fifty feet away. From a distance you realize it's not about the woman at all. It's actually a portrait of president Abraham Lincoln. It's mind-blowing artistry. The woman disappears into the larger picture. Why would Dali want to make a portrait of president Lincoln from a nude woman standing on a veranda? Who knows? The guy was nuts. But that's not the point.

The point is, things are not always as they appear. God's supernatural power comes through a very unexpected source—one that is hard to see because of our pride. It is only administered through human weakness. We need to step back and examine what our activities say about who our faith is in—ourselves or God. Christian activity is so often blindly fueled by human strength—and therefore is powerless.

When it comes to the gospel, perspective is everything. Gospel clarity can easily give way to the default of what we grew up believing—what we still believe when our mind is on autopilot—that we can make ourselves better. It's the same individualistic lie the world promotes: do better, discipline yourself more, choose your own destiny, be somebody. But the gospel is a gift given to sinners who humble themselves before an almighty God, surrender to His plan, and gratefully receive the sacrifice He made on the cross to pay for their sins. It doesn't demand the spotlight—it doesn't demand anything.

We aren't here to make a name for ourselves or compete for the Most Capable Christian award. Our purpose is to worship Christ. James commands us to "not be deceived," to "resist the devil" and "come near to God" (James 4:7–8). Instead, in the pursuit of self-preservation and self-glorification, we often find ourselves resisting what God is doing in our lives and instead coming near to (believing) the devil. God frustrates the plans of prideful, self-righteous people. One of the most time-consuming lessons He teaches His children is to humble themselves, patiently trust Him, and stop striving in their own strength and with their own wisdom to achieve things He isn't even calling them to.

The Power of God

When we think of supernatural power—we imagine things like being able to move objects with our mind or performing miraculous healings in front of masses of people. Perhaps images of Acts chapter 2 come to mind where the Holy Spirit descended in a violent wind and landed as tongues of fire on the believers there. That's the kind of power we are interested in and we want to know how to get it.

Somehow we are not interested in the kind of power that puts to death our selfish ambition. But that is exactly what was so powerful in the second chapter of Acts. Those believers lived by faith, loving each other with reckless abandon. They had no concern for their own lives. The same Holy Spirit empowers believers today who don't quench Him with their pride. We are so preoccupied with healing bodies, making a name for ourselves, our own giftedness, and mystical signs that we cease to be amazed at the miracle of a repentant sinner. No, we're bored of that—we want the kind of power we want when we want it.

What about power over sin? If I ask myself whether I hate my own sin or my neighbor's more, I would have to answer . . . my neighbor's, hands down. If only I could see my sin as clearly as I can see others' and defend others as easily as I defend myself. Humility comes through seeing our sin clearly, hating it more than anyone else's, and then repenting of it and believing the Lord has taken it away.

We can spend so much time hiding our failures we cease to understand it is our failure that reminds us of our *need* for Christ. When we fall into sin, we think there is a long road of penance back to Christ. The truth is, when you fall, you are only one repentant prayer away from being closer to the Lord than you have ever been.

We don't have to always live like yo-yos, sometimes abiding and sometimes repenting. Galatians

> "THE TRUTH IS, WHEN YOU FALL, YOU ARE ONLY ONE REPENTANT PRAYER AWAY FROM BEING CLOSER TO THE LORD THAN YOU HAVE EVER BEEN."

5:16–18 encourages us to be stabilized by the Spirit (that is, remain connected to the Vine) in order to resist our sinful desires and remain in joyful fellowship.

> So I say, live by the Spirit, and you will not gratify the desires of the sinful nature. For the sinful nature desires what is contrary to the Spirit, and the Spirit what is contrary to the sinful nature. They are in conflict with each other, so that you do not do what you want. But if you are led by the Spirit, you are not under law.

The concept of humility is easy to understand (we don't need a theologian to spell it out) but impossible to apply apart from abiding in Christ. When we are not abiding in Him, we become selfish in our marriages, in the church, and in the world. We begin to try to control our circumstances, the people around us, and our own behavior—unsuccessfully—rather than surrendering to the Lord and trusting in His sovereign control.

The Lord had every right to destroy mankind at the first sign of rebellion, but in His mercy, He humbled Himself, allowing us to live and have the opportunity to be reconciled to Him. Jesus could have arrived in Jerusalem in all His glory. Everyone would have recognized Him as God. They would have been consumed by His holiness, and forced to bow to Him. Instead, because of His mercy, He clothed Himself in flesh and revealed His identity through miracles. Their response? They killed Him as He willingly yielded. The power that came from that kind of humility brought about redemption for mankind. There is power in our lives as well when we humble ourselves under God's mighty hand and entrust Him to lift us up in due time (1 Peter 5:6).

Christ finished the work of redemption on the cross. That's what He meant when He said: "It is finished" (John 19:30). Resting in that truth and actually believing it is sometimes the believers' greatest struggle. It's too good to be true. But Jesus's command to us is to believe in Him and love each other—even *that* cannot be done without Him.

It is difficult to talk about what it means to abide in Christ without defining it with some activity. You must experience it to understand it fully and that I cannot give you. I can tell you the Lord is faithful to teach you what it means to abide in Him—your response, superwoman, is to believe.

Making it Stick

- The crowd mocked Jesus as He hung on the cross, saying, "If you are the king of the Jews, save yourself" (Luke 23:37). The truth is He could have saved Himself—*but at the expense of saving others*. The power to save us came through Christ's willingness to *not* save Himself. What areas of your life are lacking power because you are busy self-saving rather than yielding to the power of abiding in humility?

- Jesus said in Matthew 16:24–25, "If anyone would come after me, he must deny himself and take up his cross and follow me. For whoever wants to save his life will lose it, but whoever loses his life for me will find it." Examine your relationships. Is there anyone you love or seek approval from more than Christ? Do you need to humble yourself in any of your relationships now? Do you need to forgive or ask for forgiveness, set anyone free from your expectations, communicate, or confront sin?

ACKNOWLEDGMENTS

I would like to thank my husband Arnie for his kind leadership, his careful examination of this book, his eagle eye in the editing process, and his loving support and encouragement. I love you.

I would like to thank my kids, Brock and Paige, for being my greatest joy on earth.

I would like to thank my pastor Byron Yawn for encouraging me to write and teach on this subject, for collaborating with me on this project and contributing to it, and for faithfully pointing our congregation back to the gospel.

I would like to thank my agent Patti M. Hummel (President/Agent, Benchmark Group LLC, Nashville, TN) for believing in me and in this work, for never giving up on it even when I was ready to, and for all of her encouragement and counsel.

I would like to thank my editor Jamie Chavez who painstakingly edited this manuscript to make it readable without losing my voice. You are one gifted woman Jamie. Thank you!

Finally, I would like to thank the women of Community Bible Church for their service, their patience with my intense personality, and their partnership with me for the gospel. I am so blessed by your spiritual gifts, encouragement and friendship. I have never enjoyed such genuine fellowship with women as I have with the women at Community Bible Church in Nashville Tennessee.

Great crockpot recipes

This is my desire (↓song)

song
Draw me close to you